A Mother Like Him

The Practice of
Merciful Mothering
…If Jesus Had Been a Parent…

Mary Anna-Louise Gothi

Dedication

To my precious husband, Dave, you have been my rock and my champion. Thank you for loving me so well and for believing in me when I didn't believe in myself. Thank you for never letting me give up when the goal seemed so far out of reach. I love you with all my heart.

To my children…those born to me, those who joined me later and my in-law kids… you are God's gifts to my heart! I am forever grateful for the joy of loving you and celebrating life with you.

To my parents, Chaplain Sam and Anna Ruth Graves, you were my role models of loving mercifully and celebrating life. Thank you for being Jesus to me.

AMLH Endorsements

This is a beautiful book. Mary Gothi brilliantly applies the loveliness of God's mercy to our own parenting. Inspiring, uplifting, and deeply moving.

Gary Thomas, Author of Sacred Marriage and Sacred Parenting

We are honored to be a part of this book, as Mary shares our stories, both as parents and as a son who needed a merciful parent. We have known Mary for more than 2 decades and have seen her in action as a parent and grandparent so we trust her to be authentic and encouraging in this book.

Jud and Lori Wilhite, parents of 3, pastors of Las Vegas Central Christian Church and best-selling authors

We wholeheartedly endorse Mary's beautiful new book "A Mother Like Him." Right from the start, Mary will capture your heart and bring hope to Moms who are struggling! Every chapter is chocked full of real-life stories by Moms "in the trenches" of parenting. Mary weaves these wonderful stories with God's Word, and her own journey and wisdom as a Mom. A Mother Like Him" empowers Moms to lean on Jesus to pour His loving mercy out through them, even when they feel at the end of their parenting rope!

We agree that "Unconditional, merciful love removes all of the unrealistic expectations we can never meet. Merciful mothering loves us as we are!" (from Chapter 5)

Hans and Donna Finzel, parents of 4, Founders of HDLeaders and best-selling authors

This book is a treasure trove. In A Mother Like Him, Mary Gothi weaves together story (her own and others), Biblical principles, and the kind of real-life wisdom that comes from experience. Encouraging and tender, Mary's writing evokes the experience of sitting with her over a cup of tea. Readers will come away with practical parenting principles, but perhaps more importantly, with the reassurance that God sees them and is with them in the journey of mothering.

Sarah Cowan-Johnson, mother of 2, best-selling author and Christianity Today's "Best Marriage and Family Book of the Year," Teach Your Children Well: A Step-by-Step Guide for Family Discipleship

As someone who struggles to extend grace and mercy in my closest relationships, A Mother Like Him was the gentle guide I needed to rewrite the narrative with my children. Mary has a way of illuminating biblical truths with real-life stories from her parenting journey and those of her ministry friends around the world. From tantruming toddlers with unique personalities to wayward teens struggling with addiction, this book covers it all and shows us that in every age and stage of parenting, the absolute best we can offer our children is God's heart of mercy. In a world where hurry often flatlines our attempts at responding with grace, this is a much-needed resource for every parent "in the thick of it." As I was editing, I found myself returning to the manuscript again and again for a sweet dose of encouragement from a mother gone before me.

Jenna Kruse, mother of 3 and author of Disney and the Gospel

A Mother Like Him was such a blessing in my parenting journey. Mary does an amazing job of capturing how to parent like Jesus with grace and mercy. We are never going to be perfect parents but she captures the essence of Jesus's spirit in this book by giving ourselves grace as parents too. There are so many tools and takeaways from this book that I have implemented and it has forever changed my perspective and attitude towards parenting. Forever grateful.

Taylor Lindemann, mother of 3 and Children's Pastor, Mercy Road Northeast Church, Indianapolis, Indiana

In the book Mother Like Him, Mary Gothi writes about how to raise life's greatest blessings with the Mercy of God, with the same mercies He has lavished upon us. As a mother of 4 young children, I really appreciated Mary using the scriptures to powerfully communicate the truth about parenting. Also, I am thankful for the stories that reminded me that no matter what kind of parents I had, or the parent that I have been, with the help of the Holy Spirt, I can be a parent like Him!

Anvita Elder, mother of 4 and Pastor of Prayer and Fasting, Mercy Road Church, Carmel, Indiana

Acknowledgment

To Micah and Maren, whose childhood is throughout this book, thank you for allowing others to learn from and be blessed by your stories. Micah, I couldn't do anything in ministry without your design help. You know my heart and I trust you to represent it well. Brooke and Julia, thank you for your final design vote!

Jenna Kruse, the best editor in the world! You have been so patient with my bent to be with people rather than sit alone to write. If only I could add a winking emoji... Thank you for caring so much about this book and being so determined to make it perfect. I am forever grateful!

Jud and Lori Wilhite When you were our pastor in Southern California, you encouraged me to write. Thank you for being the catalyst that made this book happen, for allowing me to share your own stories and for being our family when we were at Crossroads together.

Gary Thomas Thank you for supporting this project with your words of encouragement and for sharing this message to far more parents than I could ever hope to reach without your help. You are an inspiration to us!

Hans and Donna Finzel I am so grateful for our decades of friendship and sharing your story (Donna) in this book. Thank you for ALL the conversations about my writing and for pushing me to get this book out there.

Lisa, Colleen and Carey, my Young Life "girls." Thank you for praying for this book, for reading chapters and being so excited about it. Thank you for loving me all these years and trusting me as we shared parenting challenges and adventures!

To my Huddle (Taylor, Robyn, Christy, Rachel, Sarah) and my other readers (Rebekah, Desiree, Anvita) Thank you for trusting me for parenting advice which crystalized what I believe and teach, for 1,000% cheerleading this vision. Taylor and Shalonda, you gave me the opportunity to teach and you challenged me to believe God has much in store for A Mother Like Him.

Anvita Thank you for praying over this book and reminding me that the enemy is a liar...that it only matters what God thinks!

Chris Ferebee, our Sunshine Ministries attorney and dear friend Thank you for telling me to keep writing when I wanted to give up, for believing for 2 decades that I had something worth saying. Thank you for guiding me in this process!

To all who allowed me to tell your story to give parents hope or contributed to this book in other ways, I am #soincrediblygrateful. Jud, Lori and Emma Wilhite, Josh McDowell, Tisha, Kristine, Shane and Rachel, Allison and Abbey, Rashad, Mercy, Laurie, Stefan, Denise, Raechel, Sarah, Donna, Ben, Jaden, Myla, Micah, Brooke, Maren, Connie, Denise, Hannah, Father Len Cowan, Lisa and Alexis

To my Mercy Road Church family....too many of you to list here, but you know who you are. You empower Dave and me to be all God created and calls us to be. This book is just part of that and we will always be so grateful God led us to you. You are HOME and we love you all so much!

To all my leader and alumni wives of The Significant Marriage around the world, I am so incredibly grateful for your words of encouragement and prayer covering throughout this process. Thank you for believing in the message God gave me to share with our couples who are parents. As this book and the seminar are translated into the languages of the countries where we serve, it is my prayer that the message will continue to be "honey to the soul" of every parent who reads it.

About the Author

Mary Anna-Louise Gothi, a psychotherapist with graduate degrees in counseling and clinical psychology, has been counseling, coaching and teaching couples and families since 1978. She has 4 grown children and 7 awesome grandchildren, whom she considers the greatest joy of her life and her most significant impact in the world. With her husband, Dave, she founded Sunshine Kids International, partnering with an orphanage school in India. They also founded The Significant Marriage, a global ministry on 6 continents that teaches engaged and married couples how to protect their relationship so that they can discover their purpose and live on mission to make a difference in the world.

To contact Mary, please visit
www.TheSignificantMarriage.com
and www.SunshineKidsIntl.com.

Contents

Introduction

What Does It Mean to be a *Mother Like Him?*

"Be merciful, just as your Father is merciful."

Luke 6:36

When I was a clinical psychology student at Wheaton Graduate School, I wrote a paper on the healing power of biblical mercy. The concept of mercy as mandated in the Scriptures has become a mantra of mine, one that I passionately believe can change families if they take it to heart and apply it to their relationships. Although there are several hundred references to mercy in the Bible, I have never heard a sermon in which the sole focus was this attribute of God. This amazes me because, as I have continued to explore the meaning of the Lord's mercy in my own life and his call upon me to offer that same mercy to others, I have found it to be a life-changing experience. **In the mother-child relationship, I believe mercy can profoundly impact how we parent our children.**

Before we can choose to offer this mercy, it is helpful to understand what mercy is. As technical as this may sound, here are the facts: Merriam-Webster's Dictionary says in part that mercy is 1) compassion and 2) a blessing. It stresses goodwill, shown in "a tolerance of others and generous forgiving or overlooking of [one's] faults or failures." It goes on to say that it "is synonymous with...grace, implying compassion that forbears punishing even when justice demands it."

The Theological Wordbook of the Bible says, "Mercy stands in the Old Testament for the Hebrew word 'chesed' or loving-kindness. It signifies the forbearance (patience) of God by which he keeps his covenant with Israel despite their waywardness and slowness in keeping his commandments. It also is used as 'racham' which describes God's tender compassion and pity for man in his helplessness and weakness." The Theological Wordbook also lists the word "chanan" as being interchangeable with mercy. "'Chanan' describes God's generous and kindly disposition. It is not forgiveness—it is the motivation behind forgiveness."

In the New Testament, the Greek word for mercy is "eleos," which means pity and mercy shown toward repentant sinners. Baker's Dictionary of Theology says mercy is a "communicable attribute of God, expressing God's goodness and love for the guilty and miserable. It includes pity, compassion, gentleness, and forbearance. It is both free and absolute (covering all areas of life.) God's mercy to man requires mercy on man's part (Matthew 8:23-35)."

In other words, **God expects that I extend the same mercy he has shown me to others.** Luke 6:36 says, "Be merciful, just as your Father is merciful." Period. It doesn't read, "if you feel like it," "if you had a great day," or "if this person has been merciful to you." It is a mandate, pure and simple, with no reward promised, and as impossible as it may seem, God never asks anything of us that he doesn't also empower us to do.

God desires that we **extend this mercy to our children**—those precious people in our lives who are often, as Baker's put it above, "guilty and miserable," "helpless and weak," and in desperate need of our compassion, gentleness, and forgiveness. The Old and New Testaments frequently connect mercy to righteousness. Mercy is an intertwining of righteousness and love, often described as "chesed" or steadfast love. In this, there is a mutual relation of rights and responsibilities, as God's mercy is required because of his covenant with his people. God expects mercy from us. This is the "chanan:" the motivation behind the mercy. As parents, we are in a lifelong covenant with our children: to love them, protect them, believe in them, and support them. This scriptural mercy is also once again described as loving-kindness, denoting an affectionate kindness produced by deep-felt personal love. Lamentations 3:22-23 says, "The Lord's loving kindnesses indeed never cease, for His compassions never fail. They are new every morning." As parents, we understand there is something to be said about starting afresh every day, no matter what has happened the day before!

You may be asking yourself...

Is Jesus really asking me as a mother to show unfailing compassion and consistent, loving-kindness to my children? How about when I am exhausted and haven't had my own needs met?

Is he really expecting me to be gentle and patient when I would rather scream or on some days even run away to a different life?

Does he honestly expect me to forgive when my heart has been broken again and again?

If I believe the Scriptures to be true and accept the mandate for living that God has given me to follow, then the answer to all of these questions is "YES!" **Because he dwells within us, his Spirit is able to be merciful through our spirit—all he asks of us is to have a willing heart and trust him. With his help, it is possible to be "a mother like him."**

Chapter 1: Merciful Mothering Seeks to be Consistently Compassionate

"The Lord's acts of mercy indeed do not end, for his compassions never fail.

They are new every morning..."

Lam. 3:22-23 (NASB)

When my daughter Maren was a child, she was anything but timid. She tackled challenges with unwavering persistence as long as she could see the reward. When she was only three, we went sledding at a local school. Though the hill was high, she chose to go down alone. At the end of the ride, she attempted to get herself and her sled back up to the top. As her tiny body exerted more effort, the rope kept slipping out of her mitten, sending the sled sliding back down the hill. As I watched from the top, I agonized, wondering if I should go rescue her. I needn't have worried because when she finally started making headway, she looked up at her dad and me and said with a huge smile, "I'm makin' it! I'm makin' it!" Allowing Maren to struggle through that moment proved worth it. I knew right then Maren would take on any challenge in life and give it everything she had.

For me, being mercifully compassionate with my children means putting myself in their shoes, seeking to see the world through their eyes, and feeling what their little hearts feel. This often means putting my own agenda aside and seeing and meeting their needs instead. And those needs vary as widely as their personalities are dynamic.

That same Maren who proved to have a strong and determined spirit also displayed an extraordinary spiritual sensitivity from a young age. She was very aware of the presence of both good and evil in the world. Though we tried to keep her focus on Jesus, she seemed to have an uncanny awareness of the unseen world, both positive and negative. Being a child, this also meant her imagination could run wild. Suddenly, and often without notice, the determination we saw that one day on the snowy hill would evaporate into a sense of fear. The things unseen, or that existed in her imagination, evoked a very different response from this strong yet sensitive child of mine.

When she was five years old, I made the mistake of introducing *The Wizard of Oz* to Maren, thinking that watching this classic would be fun for her. On the contrary and much to my dismay, the Wicked Witch suddenly lived in all the places in our apartment that I wasn't—in her closet, under the couch, behind the door. For months, Maren followed me *everywhere* I went.

I could have responded with exasperation, and once in a while I did, but I sought to understand her little frightened heart. When I did, I managed to offer her compassionate mercy. According to *dictionary.com*, compassion is a characteristic of mercy. Therefore, when it reads in Lamentations 3:22-23 (NASB 2020) that "the Lord's acts of mercy indeed do not end, For His compassions do not fail," it is a double reminder of God's unending mercy toward us. "Never" is an intense word. Yet when Jesus calls people who follow him to be merciful because he is merciful with us, he doesn't qualify this command with timing or circumstances. There isn't an easy out, nor is there room for excuses. His mercy toward us is consistent, never failing. Period. It is not dependent upon perfect behavior or how he feels about us at the moment.

And yet, nights are on an entirely different level of challenge to our desire to be merciful mothers. Never having been a great sleeper, when the world of Oz opened Maren's mind to new fears, to things she imagined might exist, sleep became almost nonexistent for all of us. Every night, without fail, Maren would come into my room and wake me up, often more than once. Her room was on the other side of the apartment from ours. So she felt like she was an ocean away from the people who made her feel safe.

Some nights I was so exhausted I didn't respond with a merciful heart at all. I was grouchy and angry with Maren, frustrated that she didn't stay asleep like "other children." Just remembering those moments grieves me. But when I allowed mercy to rule in my heart, I was able to feel what she was feeling and understand her frightened heart. Looking back, I was the same way as a child, so it makes me angry at myself that I didn't always have a grace-filled response to her. I couldn't force her to sleep, nor could I make her stay in a peaceful state of slumber once there. Those things were out of my control. But I could choose to help her feel safe in the middle of the night.

As moms, we often respond to our children based on how they behave or how we are *feeling.* Jesus is merciful to us because he *consistently chooses* to respond to us in this way. As much as it may seem impossible for us, he desires us to offer this same kind of mercy to our kids. He wants us to choose consistent, moment-by-moment mercy and offer underserved forgiveness, kindness, patience, and compassion even when we wish we were far, far away from our kids. **He calls us to a higher standard because it is through this kind of compassionate, merciful love that our children experience Jesus through us.**

Marj, a family friend with a special heart for Maren, encouraged us to help our daughter learn Scripture that she could claim when she felt afraid. We took that advice and together memorized a verse that Maren recited every night before she went to bed: "Fear not, for I am with you. Do not be dismayed. I am your God. I will strengthen you. I will help you; I will uphold you with my victorious right hand." (Isaiah 41:10 TLB).

Her dad and I put a pallet at the end of our bed and a soft, child-size mattress where Maren could lie down if she came into our room at night. Just knowing she had this option gave her a greater sense of peace. Many mornings we would awaken to find her sound asleep on her little haven. As she grew, that verse remained a part of Maren's life, giving her the strength to stand against anything that caused her fear or concern.

One of the most amazing things about the Incarnation—Jesus coming to us as a baby and growing to be a man—is that he can fully understand what life is like for us. He is able to put himself in our place. Hebrews 2:17 says, "Therefore, in all things He had to be made like His brothers so that He might become a merciful and faithful high priest in things pertaining to God, to make propitiation for the sins of the people" (NASB 2020). **God allowed Jesus to experience everything he did so that he could be merciful with us!** He truly understands what it means to be exhausted and misunderstood.

Because he was never an earthly parent, it would be easy to think he can't possibly understand what it is like to be a mom of toddlers who won't give you a break, or worse—a teen who has broken your heart. But he came to live among us to experience every temptation, emotion, and frustration we experience so that when we desperately need his mercy—but really deserve his judgment—he can freely offer it because he has been in our place. He can genuinely understand the struggles we face.

"We don't have a priest who is out of touch with our reality. He's been through weakness and testing, experienced it all—all but the sin" (Hebrews 4:15 MSG). **Even though Jesus was never a woman or a mother, in his perfection, he has experienced even greater demands of a merciful heart. We can be confident he wants to help us be the parent he is calling us to be and who our children need us to be.**

Chapter 2: Merciful Mothering Is Humble and Kind

"Therefore…clothe yourselves with compassion, kindness, humility, gentleness and patience."

Colossians 3:12 (NIV)

How many of you mothers remember a time (or maybe you're currently there!) when helping your child pick out his or her outfit was seemingly the first battle of every day? My hand is raised. Unfortunately, it often negatively sets the tone for the rest of the morning. In my house, we eventually learned to pick out our clothes the night before, and *most* of the time, it curbed our tendency to battle it out during the first hour of our day.

Our choice of clothing conveys how we plan for our day to go. If it is a workday, we remember the office dress code as we rummage through our closet. If a Zoom call is on the schedule, we go the extra mile and put on the makeup. If we're having a playdate or it's gym day at school, tennis shoes are the wisest, most comfortable choice. The same is true of our spiritual lives: what we choose to wear spiritually matters! Colossians 3:12 reads, "Clothe yourselves with compassion, kindness, humility, gentleness and patience." God calls all of us, and especially us mothers, to cover ourselves with his merciful, gentle cloak so that we can offer our children what they need.

But we need to plan! If I wait until the heat of the moment to decide what I will be clothed in that day, I will often choose my own will and be dictated mainly by "in the moment" emotional responses. However, the cloak of the Spirit enables us to humbly set aside our needs and expectations to offer kindness, patience, and self-control when we would naturally respond with disappointment, impatience, or even anger.

My friends Jud and Lori had to put this cloak on one day when their daughter Emma needed some mercy. "I toloring, Mama!" Those proud words from two-year-old Emma sent her mom, Lori, running down the stairs to find out just what she meant. As she ran, Emma continued, "Daddy's 'puter boken. I fix it." Fearing the worst, Lori entered the study where she found that Emma had colored her Daddy's computer!

To understand the seriousness of the situation, one must have witnessed the artistic style Emma typically displayed in her coloring. I often cared for Emma so her parents, who pastored at my church, could go on dates. Emma was the most meticulous toddler I had ever known, and when she "tolored," she covered *every* inch of her subject rather than the random scribbling most young children do. So, in "fixing Daddy's 'puter" she had colored *every* inch of it— monitor screen and sides, keyboard, and mouse pad—with black *permanent* marker. Not to mention, Jud is an author as well as a pastor, so his study and computer are sacred territories where he spends hours writing. Panicked, Lori scrubbed the marks with nail polish remover, trying to remove the toddler artwork that covered his computer.

Now the proud owner of a "designer computer," Lori waited for Jud to come home so she could show him Emma's work of art. He walked in the door and Lori did, as Jud says, "that couple thing you do to prepare your spouse for the worst: 'Now, honey, don't be too mad....'" Expecting him to be upset, she led him into the study where Jud stopped in his tracks and took a very deep breath. It was a moment that held a great opportunity to be forever etched into the heart of a child as Emma would experience firsthand the sacrificial act of grace. But it was also a determining moment for parent as Jud hung in the balance for that split second. He would either regret his actions later or get to stand back in awe that God was gracious enough to rescue them in an instant and give him a loving response. At this point, Jud chose to humble himself and clothe himself in kindness. He looked at the computer and said, "Well, those are just love marks."

Jud and Lori discovered at that moment what it means to offer your child mercy for behavior that can sometimes bring out the worst in us. They both chose to be merciful in their response to Emma: they humbled themselves, reacted in kindness, forgave what was undeserved, and made good out of what could have been an anger-ridden scenario. When Emma is older and they tell her this story, she will understand a little of what it means to love unconditionally and to celebrate the power of merciful forgiveness.

Jesus was such a perfect example to us of this merciful, kind-hearted forgiveness. Think of the woman caught in adultery in John 8 and put yourself in her place. Can you imagine her relief when, instead of condemning and ridiculing, Jesus offered the woman mercy, telling her to "go and sin no more" (v. 11)? She had to be astounded. The impact of this mercy in her life was much more far-reaching than if she had been punished or treated with disgust. Had Jesus been angry and demeaning, she would not have been able to tell the story of his grace in her life. Likewise, if Jud and Lori had humiliated Emma for her innocent indiscretion, she would have held that anger in her heart. Instead, she was washed in the overflow of their kindness and patience with her.

We can all remember times when we wish someone had offered us mercy but didn't—times when we really needed a hug but received rejection or anger instead. The complicated thing is that our kids' outbursts and bewildering actions sometimes become our most needy moments as parents. We are not much different than them—when we are the most fragile and in need of love, we tend to act out inappropriately or angrily, often to our regret. But there is one distinction: we as parents have more tools in our social and emotional toolbox and are more capable of using them.

One of the best books I have ever read on parenting is *How to Really Love Your Child* by Dr. Ross Campbell. This book is over twenty-five years old, and I read it countless times to keep my head and heart straight as I raised my children. (The follow-up book, *How to Really Love Your Teenager*, is also excellent!) It has enriched my understanding of the Bible as it relates to parenting and also in leading others through the challenging experience of being parents. Dr. Campbell speaks of a child's emotional "love tank" that needs to be full of our love. If our child's love tank is empty—if we haven't diligently and obediently been filling it with our attention, patience, and mercy—it quickly becomes empty. When it is empty, a child cannot be at their best and *will* act out. Dr. Campbell admonishes us as parents to be sure we have filled their emotional love tank before we react to their behavior.

Keeping this love tank full isn't difficult, but it does mean daily and often moment-by-moment choosing to be obedient before the Lord in loving our kids intentionally with his love—in other words, clothing ourselves with it. This book says there are four simple ways to show your child love to keep his or her love tank full.

The first one is eye contact. Looking a person in the eyes while communicating with them conveys that they are worthy of your time and intentionality. Children have this same need, but sometimes we are so busy with daily tasks, like washing the dishes, that we don't fully listen. I practiced this so much with Micah and Maren, telling them to "look at me" when we were talking, that they began to use it on me! One day while I was busy in the kitchen, Maren, who was around three years old then, was trying to get my attention. I do not remember what I was doing then, but I will never forget how humbled I was to hear her say with her determined little voice, "Mommy, look at me!"

Eye contact initiates connection, but physical affection takes it a step further and is the second way to keep your child's love tank full. The need for physical, human contact has been proven by research over and over again as God created us to be in relationship with others. It is through loving relationships that we can experience him! Children need all of the hugging and cuddling we can give them. When my husband and I aren't giving enough hugs to each other, we know something has gone awry in the relationship that we need to get to the bottom of. It causes us to evaluate where we need to be more intentional.

Similarly, children know their relationship with their parents is secure with the help of our physical affection toward them. Children desperately need to know they are loved through our gentle touch. It is such a crucial part of the relationship we have built with our children that even though our kids are all grown up, we still don't leave their presence without hugging them, just like my parents had done with me.

The third way to keep a child's love tank full calls on your *time* as a parent through focused attention. When Jesus spent time with someone, I imagine they felt like they were the most important person in his world at that moment. Our children need to feel a healthy dose of this from us as well. Real life, as you know, doesn't allow us to spend every minute focused on our children's needs, but Campbell emphasizes what a difference it can make to a child to have time alone with us. It conveys to their heart that for that short time, no one else is more important to us—that we enjoy putting them first. This is so powerful in building their self-esteem!

Spending quality time with your kids could mean taking each of them on "dates." From the time Micah was just a toddler, we would go down to the local soda shop and talk. By the time he was a teenager, we were going to cafés for coffee or out for sushi, and we would just sit for an hour and share our day. Maren and I went out for tea to our favorite café in Vienna. (Raising them in Austria, where we were missionaries, allowed us to explore and enjoy very special places!) When she was still a young girl, we would sit surrounded by old European elegance, laughing and sharing silly stories over our cups of tea.

Today, this is still one of my favorite things to do with my adult children. **I believe they knew they were the most important people in my life for those moments, and I will always be thankful I spent that time with them.** Those memories will be forever embedded in our hearts, whereas, by contrast, I can't even remember what busy thing I had to give up in exchange for those precious dates with them. Recently, I had a busy calendar filled with appointments, but when our youngest grandson, Ben, texted to ask if we could hang out, I moved "heaven and earth" to make time for him. When my granddaughter Myla asks if we can go to Starbucks, I respond the same, so grateful that she wants to spend time with us. If Jaden, the oldest, wants to do breakfast or dinner, we will change plans to hang out with him. Dave and I would make this choice for any of our seven grandkids and give anything if all of them lived closer!

Teenagers are especially busy, so make space in your schedule to enjoy them and don't be afraid to ask for their time. Spending time with the people you love is indispensable because it shows them how valuable they are to you.

The final way to fill your child's "love tank" is through discipline. Campbell describes discipline best in that it **embodies mercy.** Jesus often uses the image of the shepherd and sheep to teach us about his relationship with us. When writing about punishment, Campbell says the shepherd never uses his staff to hit the sheep. Rather, he uses it to gently guide them in the right direction. Similarly, he says that punishment is a very small part of discipline; we should be focused on guiding. If our kids' love tanks are full, there will be less need for punishment anyway!

When I was in junior high, I attended a Christian school. As were most Christian schools at the time, it was strict, and I was always in trouble, either for my skirt being too short for my long legs or for talking too much to the boys. My dad was in Vietnam that year, and my whole world was uncertain. Not only was I going through the normal struggles of becoming a teenager, but my best friend in the entire world—my dad—was at risk, and I wondered every day if someone would come to my door to tell me he had been killed.

This reality affected me greatly, and I am sure it played a role in how I acted out. Had my dad been safe at home, things may have been different, but no one ever walked alongside me to ask me if I was hurting or to talk me through my fears. No one offered me the humble kindness and patience of mercy I was needing. When we so desperately need mercy and don't receive it, scars are left on our hearts that affect our whole lives if ignored and left unhealed by God. Sadly, so many of us can call upon occasions in all our lives when we needed mercy and didn't receive it.

Fortunately, there have also been times in my life when I am sure I deserved punishment but was offered merciful grace instead. I can clearly remember moments in my own children's lives when I had to choose to say, "go and sin no more." When Micah was eleven years old, he and his sister were arguing. They were such close friends and had played together since Maren was just a baby in a box that he would push around, so if they were fighting, it meant something serious was happening! They had been outside playing in the yard when Micah came in so angry at her that he punched the door with his fist.

Looking back, I am thankful Micah didn't instead hit his sister, but the door had small glass panes, and regrettably, one shattered! Micah was left unharmed but his emotions needed some tending. He was so disappointed in himself for getting that angry over a simple argument with his sister. After accepting the consequence of helping pay for a new windowpane, he still needed me to be merciful with him. This behavior was so unlike him that I needed to consider how full his emotional love tank was before I reacted in anger to his actions. He was punishing himself enough for his behavior. For whatever reason(s), his emotional love tank was running on empty.

Perhaps I had been too busy with graduate school and hadn't given my son enough face time, affirmation, or cuddling. Before I reacted to his negative behavior, I had to humble myself before God and Micah and take responsibility for filling his love tank. What he needed most from me was kindness and gentleness shown through a hug. He needed mercy.

Too many times, because of tiredness or busyness, we don't offer mercy to our children, and for me, those times still grieve my heart. But God knows our hearts and our desire to be faithful. At the end of the day, after the kids are in bed and we lay awake processing through the wins and the challenges, the Spirit nudges us to keep trying for the sake of mercy.

There are no excuses. To reiterate what *Baker's Dictionary of Theology* says of mercy, it is a "communicable attribute of God, expressing God's goodness and love for the guilty and miserable. It includes pity, compassion, gentleness, and forbearance. It is both free and absolute, covering all areas of life." God's mercy to us requires, in response, mercy from us toward others. Micah 6:8 says, "He has shown you, O man, what is good; And what does the Lord require of you but to do justly, to love kindness, and to walk humbly with your God?" He has shown us! And it doesn't have to spring naturally from us because God's mercy flows through us! It is his compassion, his gentleness, his patience, and his kindness that flows through us and empowers us to be merciful to our children.

When Micah was eight years old, we lived in a flat in Vienna. Having gone out for the evening, I came home to my favorite pottery vase glued back together. Micah knew he wasn't supposed to play soccer inside, but apparently, the temptation was too great in my absence, and as a result, he broke the vase. I had a choice to make! "Go and sin no more" seemed the right path. Micah had not only glued the many pieces of the vase back together perfectly but also waited in agony, ready to tell me the truth, sweating about what my reaction would be. I can just imagine the guilt and fear he experienced as his little hands worked anxiously to fit all the broken pieces in the right place before I arrived home. Micah learned far more from those tense minutes than I could have taught by punishing him. At that moment, he needed my mercy. He needed me to wrap my arms around him and tell him I forgave him. He needed me to humble myself as my "need" of a perfect vase paled in comparison to the need for relief he experienced in the safety of merciful, gentle, "loving-kindness."

Three decades later, that vase still sits in my study. It reminds me not only of Micah's love for me and his sweet spirit but also of my desire— and capability as God's child— to be a merciful mom. It reminds me to lean into my need for Jesus to flow through me in offering the kind, humble patience of mercy that my children and grandchildren, no matter their age, will always need from me.

Jud probably didn't save his "designer computer" like I did my vase, but that day will still be embedded in his long-term memory, and his merciful love will be forever embedded in Emma's heart. Both Micah and Emma are now adults who serve God and share his merciful love with others through youth and worship ministry. How we respond to our children when they don't deserve, but desperately need, kind and patient mercy from us will shape how they respond to the mercy of their heavenly Father in the future.

Chapter 3: Merciful Mothering Blossoms Out of a Healed Heart

"Do not conform to the pattern of this world, but be transformed by the renewing of your mind. Then you will be able to test and approve what God's will is-his good, pleasing and perfect will."

Romans 12:2 (NIV)

Sometimes our own childhood experiences affect how we parent. The flawed examples of our parents can either prevent us from being merciful mothers or drive us to be different than our parents were with us. I have several friends who, both as children and adults, have struggled in their relationships with their mothers. Because of what they went through, they have chosen to offer compassionate mercy to their kids. You may be able to relate to one of their stories.

When we lived in Southern California, my husband, Dave, and I were in an accountability community where we had the privilege of growing in faith together as individuals and couples. We shared our life stories to better understand the circumstances, experiences, and relationships that made us who we are as adults and know how to offer support and encouragement to each other.

Connie and Tisha had similar mothers for whom they could never measure up. Nothing they did was quite "good enough." Longing to belong and be accepted by those who gave them life, Connie and Tisha both spent many years hoping to earn the approval of their moms. Instead of compassionate mercy for their failures, however, they received criticism. For Tisha, this often also meant a withholding of love as a punishment. Because of whatever wounds they had possibly received in their own lives, Tisha's and Connie's moms seemed unable to put themselves in their daughter's place.

I watched Connie and Tisha seek God to heal the deep heart wounds their relationships with their mothers caused them. And because of that, they could offer their children the kind of mercy they had so needed but missed. When one of their children misbehaved, they didn't let them "off the hook," so to speak. However, they *did* diligently offer forgiveness and love to them. They compassionately sought to understand what their children felt that led to the misbehavior in the first place.

Because we spent a lot of time together, I witnessed them on countless occasions putting in the hard work of offering mercy to their kids, seeking to be the best moms they could be. When Connie's teenage daughter reacted to many scenarios in the frustrating way you might expect from a typical 13-year-old, Connie sought God's help. She asked him to help her remember what it felt like to be a young teenager who thinks her mom is clueless. Putting herself in Sarah's place enabled her to be more merciful in her responses. **Someday, when these children are adults, they will look back and know their moms offered them compassionate mercy and thus will be able to pass on the same to their children.**

In Tisha's own words,

My mother was a conditional show-er of love, which confused me all the more once I became a mother. Regardless, I always knew I would not allow the enemy to make her parenting style my own. [It's] amazing the lessons we learn along the way. I literally woke up every day asking the Lord how I could make my twins' lives better and be the mother he wanted me to be. I did everything [in my power and with the help of God] to be different to them — more loving, more gracious, more giving of love than she was to me.

Ironically, this came naturally to me. I probably overdid it in the area of lavished love and told them once they were older that if they were ever going to need therapy, I'd rather it be because I was too loving! (Lol.)

How did I heal? Well, truth be told, I'm still healing. But I healed by forgiving. For years, I prayed and asked the Lord to help me understand forgiveness. So often, the enemy duped me into believing I hadn't forgiven my mother when those angry feelings rose up in me. But the more I sought the Lord, the more he showed me his compassion toward ME.

This newfound understanding of grace for myself led me to consider my level of compassion toward my mother. My forgiveness began transforming into compassion for her, as I realized that she couldn't give me what she didn't have in her. My mother had been tossed back and forth between three generations of mentally ill, abusive family members who exhibited callous and unloving behavior toward her. All my mom knew as a child was abandonment. She learned to live from a place of self-protection. After marrying my dad, who was a physically abusive alcoholic, she was in survival mode once again. She didn't have it in herself to be a loving, caring mother because she was running on empty.

She wasn't a mean, wicked person; she was void of the love and acceptance of Jesus. Ironically, she taught me about God, which is how I knew him, and I suppose if we can give our children just one thing in life, it should be Jesus. Even so, she never walked in the mercies, freedoms, and love of Christ, so she was unmerciful with me. In contrast, it was the freedom and love of Christ that allowed me to parent my children with love.

When Austin was a teenager, he came to me with some horrible, heavy news—a mess he had gotten himself into. As he spoke, I wanted so badly to react and shake the 'stupid' right out of him! But the Holy Spirit quickened my heart and I heard, Remember! How you respond will leave an impression on his life. When he is a husband and a father one day, he will remember how you handled this situation. My mother would have walked away from me or, worse, pulled out my hair. But I wrapped my arms around my son (as I imagine Jesus would do to me) and told him I loved him. Two days later, he made the most heart-warming post to his friends about the love of a mother. How in the world was that possible for him to see? Only Jesus.

Today, my children seek me out. When too much time has elapsed, they get restless and tell me they need to see me. This is the fruit of the work of a mother after God's own heart, but it's also a testament to the love and mercy of Jesus toward me.

I reach out to my mother frequently via text and she does me as well. It's nothing too deep or super meaningful, as I understand now that she is incapable of it and is severely wounded mentally and emotionally. This knowledge pushes me to show her compassion and love her anyway.

Of all my friends, Raechel probably struggled the most as the single mom of four young children. New in her walk with God, she was healing from a very public, abusive marriage on top of all the wounds she received as a child from her mother. She never wanted to treat her children as she had been treated. One of her most vivid memories is standing still while her mother encircled her, screaming obscenities and telling her how stupid or bad she was. She wasn't allowed to move or respond.

As we saw in Connie's and Tisha's stories, sometimes having a bad example is the best motivation for wanting to be a good example. Somehow, God protected Raechel's loving heart because she became a mother so full of love for her children. She repented when she struggled to have the response she knew she should have when her very active children got out of control. Believing in mercy, Raechel chose, no matter how tired or under stress she felt, to put herself in her kids' place and to feel what they were feeling. I watched Raechel embrace a frustrated child with a hug when I knew she would rather have walked out the door. When she did respond mercilessly, she tried to understand where things went wrong and was always willing to ask her kids for forgiveness. **As challenging as the struggle was, Raechel sought to be like Jesus**

to her kids in the hopes that they would trust in his mercy as they experienced hers. I believe that God honored her efforts because today her four children are young adults who are thriving and have a very close relationship with their mom.

Raechel's mother recently passed away. Even though her mother never really changed in this life, the way Raechel responded to her did: her mom no longer held power over Raechel or controlled how she felt about herself. Through counseling, encouraging mentors, and her faith in God, Raechel found healing. She was able to forgive her mom, recognizing that she didn't want to have a bitter heart against someone who was obviously so wounded herself. This freed her to love her own children with renewed energy and focus, offering them the mercy she had never received.

I have another friend who exemplified the opposite of the wounded mothers I have been describing. As sure as any ministry calling from God, this friend, Denise, knew beyond a shadow of a doubt that her calling was to ensure that her daughter would never need to heal a wounded heart from her childhood.

Many years ago, Denise adopted a baby girl from China. Hannah spent the first year of her life in an orphanage, and Denise will never fully know what she experienced there in the earliest months of her life. She soon learned, though, that Hannah was terrified to go to sleep. When she finally did doze, she often awakened in the wee hours of the night in a frightened state, confused about where she was. Going to church or visiting friends was also traumatic for Hannah. Other than fear, she showed very little emotion, never smiling or responding to their expressions of love for her. She was extremely wary and observant of everything around her. Rather than force her to accept things she couldn't understand, Denise put herself in Hannah's place and decided to protect her until she was ready to explore more of the life around her.

Many of Denise's family members and friends expressed disapproval and a lack of understanding, especially as time passed, over the difficult decision she made to create a safe distance for Hannah. As painful and lonely as it was at times, Denise knew that making Hannah feel secure was the most important thing she could do. It reminded me of when my son, Micah, was a toddler and terrified of the church nursery. I asked my pediatrician about it, and he told me that if I met Micah's emotional needs now, he would be so independent as a five-year-old that it would scare me! Denise chose Hannah's heart and need for security over her own needs and the acceptance of others. She only prayed that life would someday return to normal for them again.

Choosing to lead a quiet life for Hannah's sake, Denise sheltered her from friends and family, trying to help her feel safe in this new, very different environment. It took *two full years* for Hannah to emotionally bond with Denise, to feel safe with her, and to be able to respond with love in return. This sensitive, sweet child was finally able to explore other environments and relationships without experiencing incredible fear and uncertainty.

I believe this only happened due to Denise's unwavering mercy in Hannah's life. Because Denise put herself in Hannah's place, Hannah responded to the world from the haven of merciful love Denise provided for her. She learned to trust others with her heart. She grew up to be a confident, beautiful inside-and-out young woman who excels at almost anything she tries. She is a far cry from the frightened baby that needed healing of her heart. Hannah is our goddaughter, and we couldn't be prouder of who she has become. We know that God will use her story to help her change the lives of others.

Mercy is another mother whose parenting has blossomed out of a healed heart. Based in London, she and her husband, John, are on our leadership team for The Significant Marriage. We have had the privilege of staying in their home and sharing life with their children. Mercy and John are consistently loving, merciful parents, so knowing her story, I asked her to share how she managed to be the mother she is. She says,

> *My mom grew up in a broken family with a loving dad*
> *who was torn out of her family as a result of her mother's*
> *extramarital affair. Her mother was verbally abusive. Even*
> *in adulthood, her mother continues to keep a distance, rarely*

reaching out or wanting to be part of my mom's life. My mom has had no mother figure in her life and has mothered out of its absence.

My father is an alcoholic and growing up in our house meant you walked on eggshells, not knowing his mood or if it would quickly change. My mom did her best to protect us from it, but it often took the form of telling us not to cry—to just keep going and ignore it.

I don't remember getting hugs from my mom or words of advice, just a look that told me to stop arguing back with my dad. If I messed up in our house, it was brought up repeatedly. My mom would stay silent even if she knew what I was being accused of wasn't true. Other times, she'd tell me one thing, but when my dad was around, say the complete opposite. Forgiveness was a foreign concept in my home growing up, as past mistakes always loomed over you to be brought up the next time you made one.

When I was introduced to Jesus, God opened up relationships with other women who were mothers and began to show me what a merciful mother looks like. I would come to them when I messed up, and they would point me to the Bible, reminding me that God wasn't asking me to carry the weight of feeling guilty. These women God placed in my life showed me what forgiveness looks like and how love can come into moments of failure.

God has continued to provide these women throughout my life. As I was pregnant with our first son, I feared that I wouldn't know how to be a loving, forgiving mother because I had never experienced it. I will never forget sitting across from a woman older than me and sharing this. With tears in her eyes, she leaned over, held my hands, and said, "God has given you the power to break those chains. Your mothering story does not have to be the same."

I am not perfect by any stretch, but that's where our three kids now get to see mercy at work too. Through my years of mothering, I've spoken sternly in discipline while at the same time holding my child's hand and telling them I love them even when they make mistakes. I've had my fair share of times when I've said something I realized was hurtful and asked my children for forgiveness. There are many times when mothering feels like I'm guessing at what I'm doing because I didn't have the example growing up. But as I continue to lean into God and take this to him, he opens my eyes to the vastness of his love that I can pour back out to my children.

My favorite book to read with our kids is Just in Case You Ever Wonder by Max Lucado. I can barely ever make it through without crying, as I want the words to wash over my children as much as they do for me. Just in case they ever wonder — in all my mistakes and theirs — my love for them is so vast, and yet God's love is even way beyond what they can experience from me.

You might be wondering how these moms were able to heal their wounded hearts so that they could offer their children merciful love. The journey was different for each of them in terms of timing, but the experience was similar. You may also be wondering how this fits into your own journey of motherhood, no matter what your family history looks like. Seeking a respected therapist who can help you understand what you have brought from your past into your present is a good place to start. Allowing God to heal your broken heart through counseling can free you to be the person he created you to be. Finding an older mentor, possibly a mother figure, who can walk alongside you, encouraging, teaching, and being an example to you, can also make all the difference in your ability to be the mom you want to be. Becoming part of a community of faith that goes deep and gets real will continue the process of becoming the "best you." Finally, if you are a person of faith, spending time alone with God just letting him speak to your heart, reminding you of all the good he created in you and sees in you, will be the sort of "holy ground" you need to heal fully.

As a child, one of my favorite images was of a smiling Jesus holding little children on his lap. I imagine that, as a parent, Jesus would have had the advantage of being God himself and therefore inherently merciful. With us, **he doesn't have to** *try* **to be merciful; he just** *is.* For us, it is more difficult to embrace this concept and choose to offer compassionate mercy to our kids when it has, plain and simple, been a really bad day.

One of my favorite children's books is *Alexander and the Terrible, Horrible, No Good, Very Bad Day* by Judith Viorst. For this poor child, everything seems to go wrong. As mothers, life sometimes feels like this for us, too. When we are standing in a store with a screaming child or up for the third time that night, being a merciful mom is the furthest thing from our minds—we would rather trade our kids in for a new bunch (joking) or simply go on a long vacation. Alone. **But Jesus' request of us is still the same, and he asks because he really does understand. Just as he offers mercy to us, he longs that we offer this same mercy to our children.** "So let's walk right up to him and get what he is so ready to give. Take the mercy, accept the help" (Hebrews 4:16 MSG). He knows that what he asks of us isn't easy, but *with his help,* we can offer our kids **unfailing, unending, always available, compassionate mercy.**

Chapter 4: Merciful Mothering Focuses on the Good

"Finally, brothers and sisters, whatever is true, whatever is noble, whatever is right, whatever is pure, whatever is lovely, whatever is admirable—if anything is excellent or praiseworthy—think about such things."

Philippians 4:8 (NIV)

In Luke 1:46-55, Mary, the soon-to-be mother of Jesus, praises God for his faithfulness and mercy in what is commonly known as "Mary's Song" or the "Magnificat." Because Jesus is God, everything she says about God's character also applies to her Son, and not once, but twice in this short passage, she speaks of his mercy. Of all the things he was and still is today, Jesus is consistently merciful, whether to individuals or a nation. One way he shows his mercy is that he chooses to focus on the good in us, the people he so loves. He maintains hope amid sin and chaos because he believes the best about us.

As shown above, Philippians 4:8 reads, "Finally, brothers and sisters, whatever is true, whatever is noble, whatever is right, whatever is pure, whatever is lovely, whatever is admirable—if anything is excellent or praiseworthy—think about such things." I love this version of my favorite verse because it brings emphasis with the words *"if anything..."* Paul endured incredibly difficult situations that left him reeling, just as parenthood can do. However, he found that focusing on even that *one thing* that is still excellent or praiseworthy brings God's peace, just as he promised it would (4:9).

One life-changing thing Paul gained from his encounter with Jesus was his sight. But this was more than just a physical healing. It was also a spiritual transformation where Paul began to see life through *Jesus'* eyes. Jesus became not only Paul's example of how to live but also Paul's entire life. In everything Paul wrote, he held Jesus as the center of all he believed in and chose to follow. His teachings exude the joy and power he found in Christ, and he challenges others to live as Jesus lived. Through the power of the Holy Spirit in his life, he found that no matter what happened to him, he could choose to see God and the good amid all the circumstances life brought him. As it says in verse 12 of the same chapter, Paul had "learned the secret of being content" in all situations. It didn't come naturally or easily, but he learned it, just as we mothers must learn new ways of focusing our hearts on perhaps that just one praiseworthy characteristic we see in our child.

In John 12, we see an example of Jesus' ability to see the good in people. He was at a dinner party in the home of Mary, Martha, and Lazarus when Mary took a large portion of costly perfumed oil and anointed his feet with it. Though one of the disciples became angry, Jesus set him straight by protecting Mary and recognizing her good intentions. He understood Mary could have found other purposes for this oil, but he saw her heart and the love of her actions. He focused on what was "excellent and praiseworthy" about Mary in spite of what others may have thought or said about her.

Seeing life and relationships through the merciful eyes of Jesus applies to our children as well. Paul understood there would be days when this would be difficult and, at times, a seemingly impossible choice. The reality is, no matter how much we love and rejoice in our kids, there are days when we wonder why God gave us the children he did. What was he thinking? **And yet, God gave us our children for a reason.** We have the unique and privileged task of raising them because he believes we can best help them become all he created them to be. **Choosing to see what is still "excellent and praiseworthy" amid this age-old struggle will enable us to accept them with joy and appreciation and offer them the merciful love they so deserve and need.**

I have a friend whose daughter shook to her mother's "core" all the beliefs and expectations Allison had about being a mother. Having had a painful childhood herself, Allison determined that she would be a different kind of mother than the one she had experienced. She wanted to have the perfect child who was quiet, sweet, and obedient, and she would be the perfect loving mom in return. Early on, this proved not to be the case, which drove Allison to despair, her frustration directed not only toward her child but also herself. From the time Abbey was a toddler, Allison knew her daughter was not going to fit the mold of what she had planned. Abbey was beyond outspoken, stubborn to the core, and would go into a frenzy over the littlest change in her life. In her own words, here is a picture of Allison's life as a parent:

When Abbey was a toddler, she was a runner and definitely had her own opinion about where she wanted to go. It was always, with no exceptions, the opposite direction I was going. I knew everywhere we went, I had to have a tight hold on her. One day, upon coming out of the gym, she escaped and ran as fast as her little legs could take her down the sidewalk. Because we always had so adamantly demanded obedience the first time, I didn't run after Abbey but called for her to stop, which she disregarded.

Thankfully Abbey wound up at a dead-end, and I had her cornered. I disciplined her as needed, and walked out of the little alley, frustrated that she had totally disobeyed and embarrassed me in front of complete strangers who had witnessed the incident. In particular, an older lady sat on a bench nearby, waiting for the bus. As I passed by, she chided me, saying she had five kids and none had ever run from her like that. And if they had, she would surely have spanked them. Now my blood pressure began to rise. Stemming from my own disappointment and anger at my difficult child, I let this lady have it! I think she'll never confront the mother of a small child again, or let's hope not!

Taking Abbey and her brother to the library became an act of courage for Allison. Once during "story time," they were seated in an amphitheater-style room. Abbey sat a few rows in front while big brother Kyle decided to be by himself at the top. Before five minutes had passed, Kyle became bored. He started running on the landing and ignored Allison's quiet pleas for him to sit down. Much to her humiliation, the storyteller stopped reading and asked her to stop her child from running. She feared that doing so would cause a tantrum, but she had no choice. Kyle didn't let her down either. She decided to leave as he began hitting her and screaming, knowing this would go over like a lead balloon with Abbey. As you can imagine, Abbey joined in, yelling at the top of her lungs, while Allison tried to drag them both, kicking and screaming through the sea of parents and kids.

She says of that day, "Making a fool out of myself is one thing, but having my children make me look like a fool is another. It's very difficult to find grace in a time like that. I needed to remember to breathe. It took me a year before I stepped foot in that library again!" In moments like this one, it was definitely a challenge for Allison to choose to offer mercy to her kids.

Allison and I met once for some parenting encouragement, and as she poured out her heart to me, I could feel how exhausted she was from trying to be a loving, patient mom to Abbey. As a therapist who had counseled and taught parents for decades, I wanted to offer her words of hope! I spoke with her about seeking to meet Abbey's emotional needs so that she would feel secure, but I also sensed that Allison and her husband had been doing all the "right stuff" to make sure Abbey was well-loved and cared for. As such, I encouraged her to find hope in focusing on Abbey's strengths—her good qualities—and working actively to build her up. I recommended some reads that would help her think differently about her situation: maybe Abbey needed some unique parenting because she was a unique child, not because there was "something wrong" with her or with Allison's parenting style. **Maybe Abbey didn't fit a mold because God had a special purpose for her special personality.**

After three years of extreme frustration, public and private humiliation, and heart-wrenching disappointment, Allison was literally driven to her knees, crying out to God for help. As Abbey matured, her behavior was getting worse rather than better. Allison shares:

> *Abbey had an older friend over to play, and while they were playing, she came to my husband and informed him that she didn't like her friend anymore and wanted her to go home. My husband asked what happened, and her response depicts her personality perfectly. She said, "I don't like her anymore because she won't do what I say." Remember, this is a friend who was a year older (and at five, a year is a lot), so we were surprised (and a little embarrassed) that she would be so bold to order her older friend around. But we were even more surprised that she had the guts and inclination to tell her to go home if she couldn't 'obey' her.*

Life with Abbey was definitely a challenge. But in that season of desperation, Allison decided that she could not and *would not* settle for just a "so-so" relationship with her daughter. And so, she made a choice, **a choice to let God change her attitude and heart** toward this little girl who seemed to bring out the worst in her. *She had allowed Abbey to make her feel like a failure,* and as she said, "When you are disappointed over and over and each day is a struggle, you just want to run away. You want to give up!" Rather than giving up, Allison decided to start each new day with God's help, seeking his grace and help to have his heart toward Abbey. For Allison knew deep in her heart that God had created Abbey the way she was for a reason, and she was precious in his sight!

When Paul wrote this passage in Philippians 4, he was writing from the reality of a life wracked by imprisonment, beatings, and shipwrecks. He knew what it meant to have a really bad day, yet he knew **the only way to find peace was to focus on what was** *still good* **in the midst of the chaos.** Again, that is why, in the New International Version, he sets the words apart and says, "…

If *anything* is excellent or praiseworthy--think about such things" (emphasis mine). He knew this would not be easy to do. If we are honest, there are times as parents when, on the surface, there seems to be nothing praiseworthy to be found.

Allison understood this as she humbled herself before God in her despair and begged him, *God, change me.* He heard the cries of her heart, and as she explains, "He allowed me to see Abbey's amazing qualities, and those qualities that weren't amazing I could still appreciate." Allison learned to accept Abbey as God created her, a very precocious, spirited girl with enough energy and passion to change the world!

This is where the power of this Scripture in Philippians can be evidenced in a person's life. Everyone knows that we all need encouragement and admiration. God created us with a need to belong, to be accepted, and to be significant. When criticism and rejection break our spirit, we act our worst. When we are encouraged, we want to be that person so the praise will continue. As Allison began to build Abbey up in her own heart, her mama attitude toward her changed. And Abbey responded to her by calming down, being more cooperative and respectful. As Abbey felt loved and accepted as she was, her negative behaviors began to disappear. **Allison had learned to offer God's grace to Abbey by focusing on all that is "excellent and praiseworthy" about her, choosing moment by moment to see her with the merciful eyes of Jesus.**

Allison will tell you this wasn't easy. She had to pretend, even though she didn't feel it. In counseling, we call this "acting as if" and encourage couples and families to "act as if" they are feeling something even if they don't. As they choose the correct behavior, the feelings eventually follow.

For two weeks, Allison chose to do what was right in spite of her feelings. She chose to think about what was good about Abbey and let go of all the negative things she felt about her behavior. This was painfully difficult for her as she decided that Abbey wasn't "trying to ruin her life" and that what other people thought about her daughter or her parenting skills didn't matter. Instead of seeing her as *"stubborn,"* she found her to be *"persistent"* and prayed God would use this as a strength, someday allowing her to never give up. Abbey's sensitive spirit became *"pure,"* while her unique way of thinking became *"admirable"* instead of frustrating. Her *"outspoken,"* feisty nature, often expressed in taking a stand for what she thought to be right, became *"noble,"* a trait God could use in the future. **She had to let go of everything she had ever believed to be true about parenting and do what worked with Abbey.** God revealed that Abbey needed a whole lot of unconditional love, mercy, acceptance, and on a practical level, verbal cues. Abbey needed Allison to take the time to explain everything to her in detail so that Abbey would feel safe.

Within six months of changing the way Allison thought about and dealt with Abbey, she became a different child. At the core, she was still a feisty, strong little girl, but with Allison's consistent, merciful love of her, Abbey felt free to be herself. Her negative behaviors all but disappeared. Because Allison made the hard choice to focus on what was "excellent and praiseworthy" about her, each day was no longer a painful, humiliating experience that drove her to despair. There were still *"those moments,"* but they were far less frequent. Practicing the merciful truths of Philippians 4, Allison was able to experience God's peace through each day with her child. **Because she learned to see Abbey with the merciful eyes of Jesus and appreciate all the good that he created in her, she was able to rejoice in her daughter with a grateful heart.**

Today, Abbey is a young adult, and Allison's choices made all the difference in enabling them to have a loving relationship through the years in which Abbey lived under her household. In Allison's words:

> *Abbey continues to walk to the beat of her own drum, and I have learned (over and over again) that my job is to parent her how GOD wants me to parent her, not how I think it should go. I've had to surrender things year after year with that girl. By God's amazing grace, we are incredibly close—she calls her dad and me and texts us almost daily since she lives by herself in a different state. She's learning to be an adult and thriving as much as she can.*

God places these children in our lives to teach us. It wasn't until I laid down all my expectations (which took until she was 20!) and completely surrendered her life and the way I wanted it to go that I finally found freedom. God gave me this picture through the Old Testament that if he, the best of all daddies, didn't produce children that made all right decisions (the Israelites were real hard-heads!), then who do I think I am to produce children who do it all 'right?' So we've let Abbey go, choosing to love her no matter what, and that has produced such freedom in me. It's also brought about a sweet relationship between us. We trust that God has her... We share our love of Jesus with her regularly. We accept her and also talk with her about the things that we're not happy about or don't necessarily agree with. She's our daughter, so we listen and love.

Choosing to be merciful doesn't mean you won't need to seek help or explore areas of growth with your child. There may be certain foods that trigger difficult behavior, for example. You may need to see a counselor who specializes in play therapy to look at deeper issues that may be persisting within your child or between the two of you. But the first place to start is to seek to understand what being merciful means and allow God to change your heart so you can choose that mercy for your child.

When Jesus said in Luke 6:36 we are to *"be merciful as he is merciful,"* he meant **we are to be merciful when we don't feel like it and even (especially) when it seems there is absolutely nothing in our child that merits our mercy.** That is what mercy is all about—it *is* unmerited, and yet we are asked to offer it to others. Our children especially need it from us because no one in their lives will give them the true mercy we can. When I think about my own walk with Jesus, I am sure there have been countless moments when he wanted to shake me in his frustration and disappointment. Yet, instead of judgment and anger, he continues to forgive and offer mercy because he looks at me through eyes that choose—*despite* my behavior and attitude at times—to see the good in me. **Jesus sees the best in us and simply asks that we choose,** *with his help—only with his help*—**to see the best in our children, to see them with his loving, merciful eyes!**

Chapter 5: Merciful Mothering Offers Unconditional Love

If you love someone, you will be loyal to him no matter what the cost.

You will always believe in him, always expect the best of him, and always stand your ground in defending him.

1 Corinthians 13:7 (TLB)

One of the most incredible things about Jesus is his amazing love for me—love that isn't based upon what I do or don't do, who I am, or who I fail to be. It is pure, all-encompassing, and too great for me to comprehend. This love is described in Romans 5, which declares,

"Already we have some experience of the love of God flooding through our hearts by the Holy Spirit given to us. And we can see that it was while we were powerless to help ourselves that Christ died for sinful men. In human experience it is a rare thing for one man to give his life for another, even if the latter be a good man, though there have been a few who have had the courage to do it. Yet the proof of God's amazing love is this: *that it was while we were sinners that Christ died for us*" (*v. 5–8 J.B. PHILLIPS, emphasis mine*).

Jesus loved me enough to die for me! It wasn't because I loved him, did the right thing, or made him look good. Instead, it was simply because he loved (and keeps loving) me. It isn't difficult for me to imagine that **if Jesus were to have been a parent, his children would have experienced this tremendous love that comes with no expectations or conditions.** This kind of love may sound impossible for us as moms, but Scripture gives us a lot of encouragement and guidance on how to live it out.

Many years ago, when I was a teenager, my mom handed me a 3x5 card with these verses from 1 Corinthians 13: *"If you love someone, you will be loyal to him no matter what the cost. You will always believe in him, always expect the best of him, and always stand your ground in defending him"* (v. 7 TLB). To this day, I still carry that worn-out card in my Bible to remind me of her unconditional love for me and her gentle challenge to remember what real love looks like. As a mother, this means that no matter what my children do or how they behave, I am to stand beside them in life and give them love that isn't based on their actions. Conditional love, in contrast, implies that we will be loved if we measure up. It sends the message that we will receive love if we are "good enough."

I have counseled countless people who were raised by a parent that loved conditionally, giving or denying love based on whether or not they had "deserved it" that day. Unconditional, merciful love removes all the unrealistic expectations we can never meet. Merciful mothering loves us as we are!

When I was a teenager, I heard a definition of love that has been a guide I have tried to live by ever since. I was at a Cru conference, and the speaker Josh McDowell was giving words to my broadening understanding of love—simple yet profound words that I still share every time I lead The Significant Marriage seminar because it applies to all relationships. "Real love," Josh says, "is not 'I love you if' or 'I love you because' but rather, *real love is 'I love you in spite of.'"* Merciful, unconditional love in my parenting means I can't say, "I love you if you do these things for me," or "I love you if you don't embarrass me in public." I can't say, "I love you because you are so cute" or "because you did well in gymnastics today!" Real, unconditional, merciful love means that I will say, both with words and in action, "I love you despite your disrespectful attitude," or inwardly, "I love my child even though his/her behavior is breaking my heart."

My mother used to show me this kind of love when I was a teenager and desperate to be my own person. She and my dad were very strict with me and sometimes I bucked against their rules and discipline. I wasn't allowed to go to dances or the movies, so you can imagine how it made me feel to turn down prom dates! Regardless of my legitimate reasons for feeling frustrated, it is with deep sadness that I will forever remember hurting my mom's feelings to the point where she stood at the kitchen sink and cried. This happened fairly often as I rebelled against my parents' rules. Her response to my contemptible behavior was to love me mercifully, or unconditionally, even though I was breaking her heart. Although I would someday become a much more lenient mom myself, I carried with me the ability to love mercifully because my mom had shown me that kind of love. Today, I am incredibly grateful she and I had a very loving relationship, and as I grew into an adult, my mother knew that I loved her in return.

A mother's unconditional love, though, is not just something to appreciate, as in "oh, that's nice!" Instead, it has the power to completely change a child's life, as it did in the life of our friend, Stefan. Stefan and his wife, Janelle, are alumni of The Significant Marriage ministry. They have a miraculous, redemptive story, and we are blessed to have their involvement in TSM. But I wouldn't be able to share Stefan's story with you if it were not for the unconditional, merciful love his mom, Laurie, had for him.

Throughout his heart-wrenching journey of battling opioid addiction and any other drug he could get his hands on, Laurie's faithful and loving influence in her son's life was crucial to Stefan's journey to freedom. I've asked them to share, in their own words, their story:

LAURIE

Stefan played football during his freshman year of college. The team trainer and I became friends. I told her I was worried about Stefan. Something was wrong, and I thought maybe he was drifting away from God.

The trainer gave me a verse, 2 Corinthians 6:2, that included these words, "Today is the day of salvation." I would begin to pray these words as a question each morning. "Is today the day of salvation?" If evening came and they were not fulfilled, I would say, "It's ok, God, maybe tomorrow." For five years, I prayed this prayer over and over and begged God to have mercy on my son. I began walking a circle around the university campus with a friend early in the morning. I told Stefan that every time we passed his dorm, I would look up and say a prayer for him. The next morning when we passed his room, there was a large poster board sign in his dorm window. It simply said, "Hi, Mom." He had such a big heart. The poster stayed in his window for the rest of the semester, reminding me how much he cared and wanted me to know it.

For several years, Laurie prayed for her son and his battle with drug addiction. Near the end of this time, Stefan began to experience a supernatural breakthrough. He was still a long way from being free from addiction, including setbacks along the way, but the process had begun.

STEFAN

Like every other time I was out of pills and would get sick, I tried to think of ways to get more. This time I drove to a different doctor in [another town]. I was able to get Ativan, a prescription drug meant for anxiety—not what I wanted, but it was better than nothing. I had been fighting this addiction for so long and was exhausted. On my drive back home, I put on a station with worship music. Something shifted in the car, and I felt conviction like I had never felt before. I cried harder than ever and kept yelling, "Father, forgive me. I am so sorry." Immediately, I felt comforted.

Days went by. I was taking Ativan in small amounts to help with the physical sickness. I was at work painting when I noticed a pill bottle in a coworker's lunch bag. Something was different. For the first time, I didn't want to be tempted. I ignored the bottle and the temptation.

However, the temptation felt too strong a couple days later, and I stole the pills from my co-worker's bag. This time, I was mad at myself for doing it. From the moment in the car when I cried out for forgiveness until now, I was feeling conviction. At the time, I didn't believe it was the Holy Spirit there in the car with me that day on the way home from the doctor's office, but I know now that his presence had completely washed over me. I actually wanted to get better. In the past, I never wanted to be set free because pills gave me so much comfort. Now, I could feel conviction before God and knew what I was doing was wrong.

Stefan knew his parents were covering him in prayer, but he couldn't fully know the depth of his mom's devotion or the fervent crying out she did on his behalf. Laurie shares what it was like for her during that three-and-a-half-year battle for her son to get clean:

LAURIE

Some days, I would just stare at the sky out our front window when I knew I had no more words to pray. I would be reminded that the Holy Spirit was praying in my place with groans that my words could not express; I was so thankful for that. Some days, I would just say the name of Jesus over and over—just saying his name comforted me. It was a cry from my heart; my feelings of fear and helplessness were voiced in just uttering his name. I didn't have to explain anything. He knew it all already. It was enough. He was interceding for me on behalf of our son, and he knew what my son needed more than I did.

Sadly, the fact that Stefan was experiencing conviction couldn't eliminate the addiction on its own. He continued to struggle while Laurie continued to pray. Stefan recalls the long-standing physical and spiritual effects of his drug addiction on his life:

STEFAN

*After my senior year, I still didn't have enough credits to graduate.
I watched all my friends find jobs and move on with their lives,
but I moved into an apartment alone. I took the fall semester off
and worked construction full-time. The spring semester came,
and I decided to take more classes. My addiction was taking its
toll on my body, and I began skipping class. Because of the drugs,
I couldn't focus to do the work. After five years of college, I had
nothing to show for it and moved back home.*

*I was still receiving conviction from the Holy Spirit and knew
I needed help. I remember praying to Jesus to help me and save
me from myself, but a minute later, I'd realize he could actually
answer the prayer and not let me get more pills. So I changed
my mind and prayed for him to stay out of this part of my life
instead. This back-and-forth battle went on for so long.*

At times, Stefan's parents were so discouraged they were
tempted to give up. But then Laurie would cry out to God. Next,
she recounts her experience of the day that Stefan experienced
another breakthrough.

LAURIE

*Praying, "Is today the day of salvation?" was a positive and
heartfelt prayer and one I had uttered hundreds of times over
many years with hopeful expectation. God had already done so
much to show his love and power to us, but I was not expecting
to receive what God had in store for me next. The timing was
amazing, and I can hardly comprehend how God did it.*

*I got into Stefan's car, which I was driving on this particular
day and set down the food I had prepared for him. I turned
the key to start the car, and the very first thing that came out
of the radio was a deep and powerful voice speaking loud and
clear. The voice thundered out of the car radio with these very
familiar and long-awaited words: "TODAY IS THE DAY*

OF SALVATION!" Incredibly, it was on this very day that Stefan was asking Jesus to cover his sins. Those six words were given to me in a masculine voice—not just spoken, but so boldly shouted, as if he too knew the enormity of what had just occurred. I was shocked! Stunned! I could not believe what I was hearing! God says that the angels rejoice when a sinner repents. I think this angel shouted his joy through my son's car radio! I slowly turned the key into the off position and just sat. I shook my head and said quietly, "God, only you could have done that. Thank you."

STEFAN

My parents knew I was addicted but didn't tell me they knew. I remember feeling really sick one morning before going to work. My mom knew something was going on, but she didn't say anything at that moment. The Holy Spirit led her to be quiet and pray for me, waiting for the right time to address it. She just made me breakfast, and I felt really loved when I deserved the opposite. Since I knew my parents still loved me and I didn't feel judged, I started feeling safe enough to share my addiction struggle with them.

As author, I want to stop and note that this chapter is not a how-to but rather another example of faithful, patient, merciful mothering. Had Stefan been younger, I believe God would have led Laurie to say something in those moments. But he was a young adult, and she sensed that alienating him could cause him to shut them out completely, leaving him at even greater risk. This is where the Spirit must lead because each addiction story is different and the people going through it may respond differently.

LAURIE

Surprisingly, our love for him did not change. I know God was in that. In the hardship of mothering, I was learning a lot about

*myself and God. I too had come from a place of brokenness and
God would use that in how I met my son in his mess. Most of
my depression as a younger mom came from a feeling that I
was not good enough. I didn't know who I was: I wanted to be
liked and I wanted to be good at something. Not understanding
where my worth came from and who gave it to me, my identity
was so mixed up in pleasing other people and hoping for their
approval instead of resting in the fact that my heavenly Father
created me and loves me.*

*Regardless, he wanted me to know him and have a relationship
with him. For so long, he was waiting for me to take his hand
and let him lead me. He wanted me to trust him. I finally
realized I was not on this earth to figure out life and walk it
alone. I realized that I am his and he is mine. He knows me
and loves me just as I am. I was now seeing the overwhelming
unconditional love God has for us. You don't have to earn it,
and it does not change when you fail. It is always there.*

*Because God met me there, I was able to meet my son with
that same unconditional love. I learned all I could about his
addiction, and as I had been doing every day for so many years,
I begged God for help. My son's problem was beyond me; what
a scary and strange revelation. Our son was now in the grip of
a substance that was not willing to let go. But God gave me a
verse from Revelation that reminded me that he alone is God.
"Holy, holy, holy is the Lord God Almighty, who was, who is,
and is to come" (4:8 NIV). He was there in my past, present,
and now future. He is holy and so able to help me.*

*Upon reading that verse, I got on my knees and fell to my face
to worship him. I could rest in knowing that he is God and I am
not. I pictured those around his throne saying the words of that
verse in worship, and I wanted to worship him and say them
too. My understanding that I was powerless and not in control
of anything was hitting me hard. I was becoming very aware
that the One who was in control could be trusted. I wanted to
let go. I needed to let go and trust him. Only in him would I
find the rest I needed.*

*The day Stefan's friends first told us that he was addicted to
prescription drugs and needed help was a dark day, but it was
actually the beginning of more healing. We didn't approach
Stefan with this new understanding of what he was dealing
with, but soon after, he called me to come and pick him up
from the car dealership where he had worked for six months.
He entered the house, sat on the couch, and looked down at the
floor. He then simply said, "I can't get any more. I need help.*

After Stefan's confession, Laurie took him to addiction clinic
where he would get the support he needed. It took five years after
his friends' and parents' intervention before Stefan was free from
his addiction.

STEFAN

*When I finally decided to start the recovery process, I thought,
"This is going to be impossible." As I began to taper down,
the more I had to rely on the Lord for strength. I'd have some
withdrawals at night, but instead of looking for substances,
I would hold onto a wooden cross in my hand and just say,
"Father, help me" over and over again. Knowing that my mom
and dad were praying for me encouraged me to hang on during
the long two-and-a-half years of tapering down. Praise be to
Jesus, it happened.*

LAURIE

*I was so confused when I prayed for God to do things quickly
and he didn't. But looking back, I see his wisdom in giving us
more time to heal together. God knew giving back what was lost
a little at a time would give all of us the chance to grow and see
him work. In his time, he addressed each thing we had lost, like
fellowship as a family, and replaced it with something new—
"streams in the wasteland" (Isaiah 43:19). He knew that to give
us precious memories to replace painful ones would be much*

more meaningful than the physical healing alone. Renewing Stefan's heart while giving him back the things he lost during his addiction was a much better way, but that way would take time. In hindsight, I see that time is what we needed.

Through all this, we learned that however hard it is at the time, it is right and good to praise God in the storm. When it seems like he is silent, we learned that he is faithful. We saw how he orders circumstances to show us his power and mercy. We praise God for what he did for Stefan and our family. Our heavenly Father is truly the father in the story of the prodigal son, watching from down the road with open, outstretched arms, longing for us to come back to him. He lovingly waits for us to come home.

It took *years* of prayer, diligent intervention, and waiting before Stefan was finally free of his opioid addiction. Along the way, Laurie had to learn how to depend on God. When she felt helpless, He showed her the way.

I want to clarify here that loving mercifully includes setting boundaries and expectations for your children for right living and not allowing a child to get away with whatever they want. Neglecting this would invite danger into your child's life in so many ways. For them to feel safe and learn how to function in life someday, we have to teach our children how to live and what is expected of them out in the real world.

In my own parenting, I set clear boundaries with my teens, letting them know what was and wasn't ok. We can laugh now with my daughter about how often she got grounded. Even so, I occasionally let her off a grounding early, letting her know I hoped and expected the best of her! Just as I learned from my parents, mercy speaks volumes. Mercy heals. I wanted her to know that no matter how she behaved, she never had to question my unconditional love for her. That kind of love inspires. I put my arms around my daughter again and again in her teen years, telling her I still believed the best about her. I told her freely and often that I would always love her with my whole heart.

Being the parent of a teenager isn't easy, especially when a crisis enters the scene and life spirals out of our control. Offering a roadmap to hope, 1 Corinthians 13:7 gives us a new way of thinking and responding, a practical way to live out mercy. Just as I placed it at the beginning of this chapter, place this verse somewhere in your life so you can read it often.

I went through the often-difficult challenges of raising two teenagers, and I did so as a single mom. Sometimes I felt alone, hoping I wasn't making every last mistake. I desperately wanted to help my children be whole amid circumstances none of us expected or wanted. While it may seem trivial after the powerful story you just read, the everyday moments can sometimes be the hardest. Today, my grown kids laugh when we remember the infamous sidewalk scene where my teenage son threw his younger sister's shoe into the yard of a gated mansion and her response was less than gracious. Behind the scenes of that moment was a mom who had to fight the temptation to be merciless toward both of them.

Fast-forward to both my children now being parents themselves—my son and daughter have both experienced moments when they had to choose to express unconditional love and mercy to their kids despite their behavior. I am amazed at how well they parent them with clear boundaries and calm communication. Now that they understand the depths of a parent's love, they have a deeper understanding of all we went through together. All those years of choosing—sometimes agonizingly—to be a merciful mother have given me two incredible gifts: grown children who now inspire me to be a better person and who call me their friend.

If you are a mother struggling with a child who is difficult to love or has done something to break your heart like Stefan's mom experienced, you don't have to struggle through this alone. His heart for you is that you would turn to him as the source of:

- the love you need to offer your child, and

- the wisdom you need to know how to balance forgiveness and consequences.

God honors your obedience in opening your heart to allow Jesus' unconditional love to flow, and there will come a time when you enjoy the reward for your faithfulness. When I look at my grown children, I believe that Jesus is pleased with the adults they have become as they live out his unconditional love in their lives.

Chapter 6: Merciful Mothering Forgives What is Undeserved

"Don't worry over anything whatever; tell God every detail of your needs in earnest and thankful prayer, and the peace of God which transcends human understanding, will keep constant guard over your hearts and minds as they rest in Christ Jesus."

Philippians 4:6-7 (J.B. Phillips New Testament, PHILLIPS)

This verse, written so long ago, is incredibly relevant to the needs of parents today. Many a parent have been literally driven to their knees by love and concern for their children, especially their teenagers. They are searching for answers and desperate for change in their child's life. They are also seeking peace of mind and assurance for themselves. Parents who practice mercy with their children and forgive what is undeserved, however, find not only peace but eventually reap the reward of sharing the same mercy Jesus has shown them. That reward, evident in the story from chapter 3 of Allison and Abbey, is the joy and possibility that can come from choosing mercy. Joel 2:13 says, "For He is gracious and compassionate, slow to anger, abounding in lovingkindness."

This mercy is fully displayed in the story Jesus tells of the prodigal son. When the son returns after squandering everything the father had given him, his father could have reacted angrily and rejected him. But offering him the forgiveness of undeserved mercy, he not only welcomes him home but also throws a lavish celebration in his honor. He is overcome with gratitude that his lost son is found—his heartache and disappointment are washed away in the overflow of his merciful love and forgiveness. When the elder brother becomes jealous and angry at this turn of events, his father replies, "'We had to celebrate and rejoice, for this brother of yours was dead and has begun to live, and was lost and has been found'" (Luke 15:32). In this passage, Jesus is not only revealing to us the mercy he offers in forgiving us when we don't deserve it, but also giving us a wonderful example of what it means to be a merciful parent.

Jud, the dad with the "tolering" toddler in chapter 2, had his own story of waywardness, much like the prodigal son's. Now the senior pastor of Central Christian Church in Las Vegas, Jud became a drug addict as a young teenager. Raised in a Christian home with loving parents, outside forces and inner emotional struggles drove Jud to seek refuge in a group of friends who were making poor choices. He acted out his anger by hurting his parents in any way he could because his parents represented everything he wanted to fight against. In a sermon about parenting "prodigal children," Jud said, "I spent many years breaking my parents' hearts." Knowing Jud today, this seems almost impossible to believe, for he is a loving husband and father and a godly man of integrity. He is also the pastor of the largest church in Nevada, changing countless lives with his wife, Lori. But Jud had to fight his way through very dark years, dragging his parents with him, before he allowed God to make him into the man he was created to be in the first place, the man who became a world changer.

Jud tells his own story in the book, *Faith That Runs the Distance*, writing,

> *Before I reached out to God, my life appeared colorless and blurry. I had become a very angry person, angry at everything and everybody. So I turned to drugs, first just at parties, but soon on a regular basis. It was my way of coping with the meaninglessness and emptiness I felt inside. My family tried to reach out to me, and my true friends attempted to help. But I was like a ghost. It was the eighties, and the motto of my life was captured in Bill and Ted's Excellent Adventure," Party on, dude."*

In his first book, *It's a Wonderful Life...Really!* Jud describes this turbulent time in his life:

> *As time wore on, I was not simply "doing" drugs, drugs were doing me. They came to dominate my life. Their immediate gratification always led to despair. My life became so empty you could drive a Mack truck through the hole in my heart.*
>
> *Eventually, I became sick of the party. I entered my bedroom and shut the door at the age of seventeen. I felt so tired—tired of the lies, the drugs, the betrayed relationships, the emptiness, and the guilt. I felt tired of being tired. So I fell to my knees and surrendered to God.*
>
> *He could have replied, "Jud, you've destroyed everything I put into your life. I gave you a wonderful family whom you worried to death. I blessed you with great relationships, which you severed. I gave you friends, most of whom you betrayed or cheated. I gave you a healthy body, which you tried to destroy. You lashed out at everything I put into your path with a self-inflicting rage that came from nowhere."* **Instead, he said something I did not expect: "Welcome home."** *Two simple words, not spoken audibly, but impressed on my heart and filled with unimaginable grace and love that changed my life. I began to participate in the world's greatest drama—the kingdom of God. The sheer thrill and joy of living by faith became part of my daily life.*

I am convinced that God used the merciful forgiveness and diligent prayers of his parents to "welcome Jud home." They had learned early on that the only way they would survive these years with Jud was, as his mother, Mary, says, "to pray, pray, pray! Not just at night, but every waking moment!" During Jud's sermon on the prodigal son, he interviewed his parents. Having spent two decades of my ministry working with teens and their parents, I was so impressed by their wisdom. Jud's father, Carlos, says, "there came a time when we were desperate, desperate enough to finally let go and surrender to God, saying 'this is too big for us! We're giving this kid over to you!'" They shared that, even though there weren't instant results (they prayed for years!), and it was challenging to wait on God's timing, **peace began to come into their hearts through surrendering Jud to the Lord.**

God began to work in their own hearts and lives through their prayers for Jud. The more they stayed in prayer, the closer they grew to the Lord and the more empowered they became to offer merciful forgiveness to Jud. They turned to their Christian friends who prayed with them and let them know they were not alone. When your child is struggling, this kind of support system is critical in helping you have the attitude God wants you to have and in giving you hope that God will be faithful to answer the cries of your heart.

Believing that if you "train up a child in the way he should go, even when he is old he will not depart from it" (Proverbs 22:6), Jud's parents tried to live a life of integrity before Jud. They believed he needed to see that their faith was real to them. They sought a mentor for Jud, knowing that if he wouldn't talk to them, he might talk to someone else who could share godly instruction and wise counsel. Whether or not your child is struggling, pray for and seek a mentor for them so they will have a relationship with someone they (and you) trust.

I am sure his parents were in agony during those painful years of Jud's rebellion and drug addiction. Their hearts were broken, and they probably wondered at times why God wasn't answering their prayers. **But they never stopped offering Jud grace and mercy.** They were **slow to anger**, and as much as was possible for them, **chose kindness** rather than demeaning criticism. Without his knowing it, **Jud was experiencing the very mercy of Jesus through the unconditional love of his parents**. They would tell you that there is no way they could have offered this to Jud if the Holy Spirit had not empowered them to do so.

Like I learned with my own children when they were teenagers, Jud's parents knew to "choose your battles," making an issue only of the things that have a moral, spiritual, or life-threatening impact.

Carlos summed up those years as "faith in God, love, and grace." Remember that "grace" is synonymous with "mercy." **If we seek God's help to offer these attributes to our children, no matter their behavior, we have a far greater possibility of seeing them restored to us and God.**

As a parent, I had to live what I always taught other parents: the relationship is the most important thing, far more important than "winning." Your relationship with your kids is not a war between two enemies, although parents of teens especially can feel this way! If your voice is loud and negative about every little issue, your child learns to shut you out and hear nothing. Even more significantly, they can no longer hear the God who is longing to have a relationship with them. **Merciful forgiveness paves the way for a relationship with God!**

Today, as I look at my adult daughter, Maren, the impact of mercy is evident in her life. I believe that if I had hardened my heart against her amid her years of teenage angst instead of offering her unconditional love and forgiveness, she would have walked out of my life and away from the God who so desperately loves her. When she was hurting and throwing angry words and hurtful actions my way, she needed his mercy experienced through me. Now an adult and gifted therapist, she has a merciful heart toward others.

I have known many teens who walked far away from God because they never experienced mercy from their mom. As adults, they have struggled to trust God because they can't believe he would love them as they are and forgive them unconditionally. When our kids have deeply disappointed us, it is so difficult to offer mercy to them. Jesus never said it would be easy. He simply told us to *do it.* "Be merciful, just as your Father is merciful.[1]" Period. So often, as moms, we can be harsh, critical, and unforgiving, expecting our children to be perfect and "represent us well" to others. Remember how Allison felt in the library? But Jesus is asking us to consider another way—the way of consistent, merciful kindness and patience that says, **"I will love you no matter what, and I will forgive you because Jesus has forgiven me."** There were probably countless

---

1   Luke 6:36

times when Jud's mother cried out to God for the strength she needed to have a right heart toward her son, a heart that would choose mercy instead of condemnation.

If your child is struggling with something significant like an addiction, offering mercy doesn't mean you don't seek practical help. Parents in this situation need to explore the options of recovery programs available to their child and find a support group of people facing the same issue. Knowing that, as a parent, you are doing everything you possibly can but leaving the results to Jesus in prayer will give you peace while waiting for change.

As difficult as it was, Jud's mother followed the example of Jesus. When Jesus was on the cross, the thief beside him had a repentant heart, acknowledging who Jesus was and recognizing that he deserved to die. Even though he deserved punishment for his crimes, Jesus was merciful to him, saying, "Truly I say to you, today you shall be with Me in Paradise" (Luke 23:43).

For us mothers, our hearts' desire for our children is several-fold— to raise a child who is whole as an individual, who has a loving relationship with us, and who accepts a relationship with his or her heavenly Father. Whether or not they feel unconditionally loved by us can make all the difference. At times, this will *only* be possible with the supernatural help of God. **Following the call of Jesus to be merciful, while symbolically laying our children at the feet of Jesus, frees us to forgive over and over again when it is underserved.** It allows us to love them with his merciful, unconditional love. While it isn't easy, God makes it possible.

Chapter 7: Merciful Fathering

*"Be completely humble and gentle; be patient, bearing
with one another in love."*

Ephesians 4:2 (NIV)

The first time I ever taught the concepts of this book, I was in Latvia where we have a strong presence of The Significant Marriage. Our leader Kristine often asked me questions as she sometimes struggled to parent her four children. Because she was mostly raised by her grandparents, she questioned her ability to show love properly to her own children. I had the privilege of watching Kristine raise her kids. Even though she doubted, I knew she was a wonderful, loving, affirming mom—very different from how she had been raised.

Like so many children raised in a formerly Communist country, Kristine's parents seldom told her they loved her because work was their purpose and it wasn't part of the culture or system to show affection to your children. Children raised in Communist countries were often dropped off at a nursery for the week, only seeing their parents on weekends. Under the leadership of a Communist regime, being a good "worker of the state" often meant allowing someone else to raise your children so you could focus on your job. Kristine was raised mostly by her grandparents. As she learned the concepts of merciful parenting from me, she asked me to share the same truths with her friends. After leading a parenting seminar for them, one dad came up to me with tears in his eyes. He explained that because his mother had been abusive, he had no idea how to be a loving father. He frequently asked God to guide him as he parented his young son. Tears filled my eyes too as he said, "Everything you just taught confirmed what God has been teaching me about loving my son. Your words are honey to my soul."

And so, I hope my words are "honey to the soul" of every dad who reads this chapter. I wrote this final chapter specifically for dads because, even though this book is for mothers, every part of it also applies to fathers. I would be remiss if I wrote this book only for moms, because they are only half of a child's developmental equation. Numerous research projects have proven that a father has an equally significant impact emotionally. A loving dad builds self-confidence while offering a place of safety and someone to emulate.

While in the presence of my own parents, there was never a time when they didn't tell me they loved me or put their arms around me in a hug. I can still picture my daddy with his outstretched arms welcoming me, and I can "feel" my mom's hugs where she swayed side-to-side as she held me. It was all I knew! There was never a doubt in my mind that they loved me. As a child, I thought this was how all parents showed love to their children. When I became an adult and eventually a psychotherapist in ministry, I learned through hearing the stories of countless clients that sadly this is not the norm. I discovered how incredibly blessed I was to have parents who weren't hesitant to express their love for me.

Our society sometimes assumes that the love of a mother is what a child needs most. Still, a father's unconditional, merciful love is just as life-giving and critically needed for a child's emotional, intellectual, and social development. My father will always be *Daddy* to me, no matter how old I become. I was his "Goldilocks," his baby girl, and he was one of my best friends in the entire world. He was playful and affectionate, making sure we celebrated life together. I knew beyond any shadow of a doubt that not only was I loved but **life was meant to be celebrated with those we love**.

Even when, as an Army chaplain, my father had to be gone for long periods of time, he would still strive to be present. Junior high can be a daunting experience for any kid, but I spent one of those years with my dad halfway around the world as he served in Vietnam. Years later, I would learn that because he was so committed to his men, rather than remain safe in his chaplain's tent, he was known to crawl on his belly to comfort a wounded soldier or pray with him as he lay dying in a rice paddy. For so many reasons, he will always be my hero. I was terrified of losing him the entire year he was on active duty in Vietnam, and since we didn't have FaceTime or emails, we had to wait for letters. It was agonizing. I acted out and was often in trouble at school and in my youth group. I went to a very strict Christian school where, at that time, rules were more important than a child's heart so I was often in trouble. How I wish I could put a smiling emoji here! At my church's weekend youth retreat, I convinced a friend to go with me to the boys' cabin in the middle of the night to play cards. Of course we got caught, but I strategically planned the escapade on the final night so that the leaders couldn't send us home early.

Decades later, I saw these youth leaders at my mom's memorial service, and they said to me, smiling, "Well, it looks like you turned out okay!" People had apparently wondered what would happen with me! The point is, **without my Daddy, I was hurting.** My emotional "center" was gone, and I was so fearful that he wouldn't return. My poor mom did the best she could to love and encourage me. My Aunt Widi, whom we lived with, even built a cool room in the garage for me. But it wasn't enough to fill the void. Needless to say, when my daddy safely returned from the war, it was one of the best days of my life.

Dads, you are important! The truths of this book that apply to merciful mothering also apply to merciful fathering. Many excellent books are written just for dads, and I hope you take the time to read them! But the most helpful thing I can offer to the parents reading this book is to share real-life examples of dads living out merciful parenting in each of the ways highlighted throughout the previous chapters. I will give examples from several friends who have had a father who exemplified the truths of Philippians 4:8. My prayer is that these examples will spur you on to be a father like him.

If you are a step-dad reading this, I want to share an important message especially for you. You figuratively "stepped" into a parental role that will be challenging and sometimes difficult, but it is critical that you understand how significant you are to these children who have been gifted into your life.

I speak from personal experience since ours is a "blended family." Sometimes life happens in a way we don't expect or choose, but God is able to redeem and restore what was lost. I will be forever grateful for the loving, wise stepdad my husband, Dave, has been to my two children. He "stepped" carefully into a family of three hurting people who needed a lot of grace and understanding. With his gentle spirit, he simply offered friendship and wise counsel. My kids learned quickly that they could depend upon him to be there for them. Faithfully present, he would listen, encourage, offer correction when needed and, especially, celebrate life with them. He honored their dad and the importance of their relationship with him while also giving them unconditional love and acceptance. I am sure that offering mercy to them wasn't always easy since they were teenagers at the time (smiling emoji), but through the years, over and over again they have thanked him for the loving father he has been to them. As a stepfather, you have a special opportunity, in the midst of painful circumstances, to help your child become all God created them to be. Your intentional choice to be a merciful dad can only empower this relationship! Whether forgiving what is undeserved or simply choosing to be kind, as you allow God to direct your heart, you will experience joy and make a difference in their life.

A Merciful Dad is Consistently Compassionate

When Dave and I got married in 1995, we moved to Massachusetts where I had the privilege of knowing Father Len Cowan, the Episcopal priest of the church we attended during the five years we were in New England. I observed the gentle dad he was to his daughters, so Sarah was a perfect person to interview for this chapter.

Sarah shares,

I always felt secure. My dad was a safe person to be myself around because he was not controlling but rather grace-filled. When I was a teenager, I dyed my hair an outrageous color while at a friend's house. My dad just laughed about it. This freedom to be myself has enabled my sister and me, as adults, to believe God's rock-solid love for us. This is a direct result of my earthly father's love for us. I never felt unworthy because my dad's love never wavered for me. It was so consistent, so constant.

My friend, Donna, who was a missionary with me in Austria, says about her father, a pastor and author, Mark Bubeck,

Daddy's arms were the safest place on earth! As a little girl, I remember the security I felt whenever he would hold me in his arms. If I was hurt or sick, Daddy was always nurturing and comforting. His discipline was from a place of compassion, and he would even teach me that the correction I was undergoing was in my best interest. Of course at the time, I didn't love the pain of the discipline, but he taught me the truth of this verse: "No discipline is enjoyable while it is happening–it's painful! But afterward there will be a peaceful harvest of right living for those who are trained in this way" (Hebrews 12:11 NLT).

My strongest memory of the safety of Dad's consistently compassionate and loving arms was when I was a senior in high school, and my boyfriend broke up with me. I was devastated, thinking this boy was "the one" I would marry someday. I ran out of the house to a nearby park to walk and cry. I felt hopeless and angry. But then it dawned on me where I really wanted to be—in Daddy's arms! I ran home and went right down to the basement, where I knew my dad would be studying for his Sunday evening message. I fell into his arms and told him all about what had happened. Daddy held me, listened, let me cry, and then prayed with me. Even though it took a long time for my heart to heal, I remember feeling hopeful after running to my dad. I look back on that, knowing that my self-image and security were on a solid path because of my dad's compassion.

A Merciful Dad is Humble and Kind

I share the story of Donna's father because we had the privilege of having very similar fathers—loving men who were humble servants of God and celebrated life with their families. They also taught us to give our lives away. Our dads were friends too because they had so much in common as pastors who were passionate about leading people to a faith in God. When I asked Donna if she was willing to share about her father, she jumped at the chance to talk about her love for him. Not only was he an example of compassion, but he was also filled with humility and kindness.

In Donna's words,

I'm eternally grateful to God for my Daddy! He was a highly successful pastor, counselor, and author, with hundreds of people constantly clamoring for his shepherding care, yet I knew his family was his priority. I honestly don't remember him ever being angry or abrupt, even though he must have been exhausted from the great demands of the ministry. He always exhibited humility and kindness to me.

A physical giant of a man, Daddy was tall and strong. He stood out in a crowd, and one elementary-aged friend thought he was a senator! I was proud of him, but even in all this, my dad was never egotistical. He respected every person as an equal and treated everyone—including the poorest and weakest—with great love. He visited the sick in their homes and in hospitals— even taking us with him to visit and pray with those in need. This spoke volumes to me as his daughter.

Even when he would discipline me, I never doubted his deep love and affection for me. He accepted me just the way God made me. His strong discipline was always tempered with great kindness—never belittling me. He called me his "pixie girl," a name that still fills my heart with joy whenever I remember it. His love was the solid-rock foundation of my life, as he modeled the love of Christ to me day by day.

*One of the most powerful examples of my daddy's humility
was the way he (and my mom) exhibited the love of Christ
and the fruit of the Spirit behind the closed doors of our home.
What people saw on Sunday was what we girls saw at home.
Even going through a crisis in one of his last pastorates, Dad
protected those who were opposing him by never speaking ill of
them, even around our dinner table. He humbly entrusted them
into God's hands and prayed openly for them. To this day, all
three of his daughters are passionate followers of Jesus, which I
attribute to our daddy's living, breathing faith.*

*My dad's life verse was Isaiah 57:15: "For this is what the high
and exalted One says—he who lives forever, whose name is
holy: 'I live in a high and holy place, but also with the one who
is contrite and lowly in spirit, to revive the spirit of the lowly
and to revive the heart of the contrite'" (NIV). This is how
my dad saw his relationship with God—that God, in his high
place, upholds the lowly through all their troubles, and I am so
grateful for his example of reverence for the Father.*

A Merciful Dad Loves from a Healed Heart

Our friend, Rashad, graciously shared his testimony with me for this book. Rashad's story is one of utter brokenness and redemption, and this redemption shows in his parenting. As God began bringing to light the abuse he endured as a child and, as a result, the pain he inflicted on others, Rashad knew he needed to allow God to heal him. And as God changed Rashad's heart, he was able to be the father his daughter needed.

He explains,

*The more I learned about the love of God, the better I was able
to love my daughter, Genesis. I learned what it meant to love
him with all my heart, soul, mind, and strength and that I
am supposed to love others as I love myself. But I didn't know
how to love myself. Because of that self-loathing, I couldn't be
the father she needed me to be in the early years. I believed I*

was unworthy. But God healed me—he helped me love myself because he loved me as I am. I started defining love for Genesis by how God healed me with his love. To help you understand what a drastic change this was, when she was eight years old, I was a deadbeat dad. I was unfaithful to her mother and even taught my daughter how to open a beer bottle.

But everything shifted when Jesus changed my heart and my life. With God's help and my wife's merciful love and forgiveness, I started loving Genesis the way God wanted me to without expecting anything in return.

Likewise, Donna believes her dad was able to become the man and father he was because God had also changed his life:

I believe a healed heart comes only from a deep, abiding relationship with God. Although Dad had a rebellious heart as a teenager, his godly mom, my grandma, poured out her heart from her knees, praying for her son to return to the Lord. God answered powerfully, and my dad headed off to Moody Bible Institute to pursue a life of ministry.

My Dad's life was transformed and defined by his intimate, moment-by-moment walk of prayer. He literally spent hours walking and praying in the sanctuaries of each church he pastored, early in the morning, and especially on Saturday and Sunday. My father could live a healed and loving life out of his time in prayer and God's Word. This healing gave him the platform to write several books and found a counseling ministry that is still making a significant impact today.

After he raised his three girls, my dad memorized over half of the book of Psalms. Psalm 91 was another life passage for him, and God was the refuge of his heart. "I will say of the LORD, 'He is my refuge and my fortress, my God, in whom I trust" (v. 2). Dad's strength came from the power of God flowing through him to others, including to me!

A Merciful Dad Focuses on the Good

As the verses in Philippians 4 say, we are challenged by God to focus on what is good and right and true, excellent and praiseworthy, trusting him to bring peace to our hearts. I would venture to say especially when we don't feel like it, and I am sure my parents "didn't feel like it" sometimes! Nevertheless, my father was always building me up, reminding me why he loved me. It could have been partly because of his personality—he was always positive, seeing the good in others. But it was also his calling from God. He was determined to help others become all that God created them to be, which would eventually become my calling too. The soldiers my dad led to Jesus and whom he mentored so long ago still call me decades later to tell me how much they loved my parents and how my dad and mom changed their lives. My daddy saw people through the eyes of Jesus, so he always believed the best about each person he encountered.

There is a wonderful book by Gary Smalley and John Trent called *The Blessing*. If you had loving, supportive parents, this book will help you understand why their care was so important for your emotional well-being. If you had hurtful parents, it will help you forgive them for whatever was missing. If a parent never received a spiritual blessing from *their* parents, it might be difficult to impart this blessing onto their children without going through counseling for healing. However, doing so can have a powerful impact on generations to come! This book gives an in-depth explanation of the Old Testament blessing that parents imparted on their children. These blessings contained several elements: *meaningful* **touch**, *a* **spoken** *message of high value expressing* **honor** *to their child, and finally, the parent created a picture of the child's special future. These elements were based upon a responsibility and commitment to see the blessing come to fruition.* These blessings were important then and they are important today because our children (and grandchildren) need to know they are treasured and precious in our eyes. The world will bombard them with criticism and judgment. Abraham spoke a blessing over Isaac, Isaac over Jacob, and Jacob over his twelve sons and grandchildren. I am so incredibly grateful that my parents bestowed this blessing upon my life and the lives of my children and, later, my grandchildren!

This experience was also true for my friend, Sarah, with her dad. She says,

> *My dad was never critical of me, so I never lived in fear of disappointing him. Things like good grades were celebrated but not demanded or expected. He would always be intentional to compliment us. Both of my parents' conviction was to speak blessing over their children. Every Saturday night, each person would get "blessed by the rest." This blessing was about who you are, not what you can do. It spoke to our being. Today I am grown with two wonderful kids, and my dad is still a "blesser," sending me cards that encourage me as an adult. He is always affirming, thanking God for me, and constantly telling me that he loves me.*

You too can be a blesser. In the Bible, the Proverbs speak over and over about how our words either bless or curse. Too often, we allow our everyday frustrations to turn into angry words over our children. But when we put all these concepts together—leading from a healed heart, focusing on the good, and being inspired by God's kindness and compassion—we are equipped to let our words bring life to our children rather than death. From the time they are tiny until they are adults living out in the world, you have the ability to honor, build confidence in, and help your children create their future with your blessing!

A Merciful Dad Offers Unconditional Love

Shane came from a family where unconditional love was far from a reality. Before Shane was born, his parents lived in South Africa. Although he was raised in Australia, he considers his father's cultural influences to have made his family very judgmental. His dad made sure Shane knew when he messed up. Neither his mom nor his dad supported what was important to him. If he was in a bike race (he is now a world champion), he heard their voices in his mind. If he won, they'd like him more. But if he lost, they'd like him less. If he lost or placed second, they said, "Why not first?"

Shane expands on growing up in a home where love was conditional:

My mom died of cancer when I was twenty-eight. My entire family called me the prodigal son because I left, and when I returned home, they would mock me. My entire life, I learned to wall off my heart to protect myself. Dad was an alcoholic and beat my mother before they moved from South Africa to Australia. The physical violence toward my mom stopped before I was born but continued with my siblings and me. I often experienced my dad's out-of-control anger. Every weekend he would drink too much and berate my mom, yelling and screaming. Then my dad would leave in the car. As a child, I feared what his drunk driving might lead to. And so, I left after my mom's death. There just wasn't enough "relational currency" to continue a relationship after she died.

I naturally display some of my father's traits—being judgmental and forceful even when I don't intend to be. So I decided I didn't need to be around those behaviors. My mom sometimes said, "don't turn out like your dad." Even into my adulthood, my dad always responded to me with threats and shame. When I tried to repair our relationship while my youngest son was a toddler, he continued to publicly shame and mock me, especially after getting drunk at family holidays. Sadly, I decided my relationship with my dad was something that couldn't be a part of my life. I never wanted my children to witness how he treated me, nor did I want them to fear I would ever behave like him."

I asked Shane how this made him a different father from his own. He replied, "You must learn the difference between what to do and what not to do. You can know what not to do, but this doesn't mean you know what to do. The model I had growing up was defective, but the only values I know and choose to live by now were formed in me in May 1995 when I began to follow Jesus. The most significant thing that has shaped my parenting style has been exposure to the concept and doctrine of grace. Instead of earning it, I now have a Savior who doesn't hold sin against me but wants to help me out! This has given me a different way of seeing life and loving my children. It has meant changing from a worldview economy to God's view of my kids and me. I now live by the economy of gift and grace, not wages or what I earn.

My parenting model comes straight from my heavenly father and what God looks like. Exposure to different dads at church has helped me create a picture of what a loving, grace-filled dad looks like. In personality, I am a strong leader with high expectations, so the challenge has been to be merciful, to be softer, to offer grace, and to understand my own shortcomings as I strive to love my kids well.

Shane also attributed much of the change in his parenting to his wife and the mother of their kids, Rachel. Shane says,

Rachel challenged and encouraged me to softer, more merciful places, helping me increase my empathy. Grace gives you more than you deserve; mercy holds back the punishment you deserve. So, I have had to learn reasonable expectations and empathy for what my kids might understand or not be able to understand yet, to "see" through their eyes. I had to be a "junior adult" when I was a kid, but I can't expect that of my children. I've had to learn to let them be a kid.

Shane and his wife, Rachel, are an important part of our TSM team in Australia. For many years I have observed how he fathers his children—children whom I happen to love very much, so I have a vested interest! It is so obvious that Levi, Mia, and Riley adore him. It is because he is constantly showing them how much he loves them, believes in their gifts, and wants to spend time with them that they are able to share this kind of relationship. As their dad, Shane is affectionate and playful, showing them respect and kindness while always encouraging their potential. Even though he is a busy pastor, he is intentional about making time for his kids. They know beyond a shadow of a doubt that, after their mom, they are the most important people in his life.

A Merciful Dad Forgives What is Undeserved

One morning when I was a teenager, I awoke to my daddy sitting on the edge of my bed in tears. He proceeded to tell me that he had heard me cussing in my sleep. It might sound silly, but this was a big deal to him. Having come through his POW experience a changed person, he left behind behaviors he considered part of his life before he knew Jesus. The irony of this situation was that there had been times in my life when I had cussed, but it wasn't part of my language at that time! He wasn't angry, but rather deeply hurt as he said, "Baby, if you are cussing in your sleep, you are probably cussing when you are awake." I convinced him I wasn't, but I was deeply saddened to see my dad hurting. Because he loved me so mercifully and unconditionally, I never wanted to let him down!

Sarah never had to worry about her father forgiving her. Whatever she did to hurt or displease him, he was clear, *"I love you and I forgive you."* He never held a grudge but instead believed in grace-based parenting. So, Sarah never lived in fear of getting in trouble, and she too had a deep desire not to let her dad down.

A Merciful Dad Celebrates Life

Anyone who knows me will tell you that because of my personality type, celebrating life is very important to me. It is life-giving and applies not only to special occasions, but also to enjoying the "daily stuff," noticing little things that bring joy and being grateful for the different people God brings into our lives. My daddy was all about celebrating the little and big things of life and he taught me well not to miss anything but to see those experiences as sweet gifts from the "Father of light." Sarah and Donna, whom I mention above, share what this meant for them.

Sarah shares,

> *When we were little, [my dad] carved out "special days" so*
> *we could do something special with him. We got to choose*
> *how we spent our special time with him. He was fun, light-*
> *hearted, and truly loved life. I am especially grateful that today*
> *he carries this on with my children, leading them in a Bible*
> *study and taking each of them on trips alone with him to create*
> *those special memories. He treasures celebrating life with his*
> *grandchildren in the same way he did with me.*

This is such an awesome reminder that "dates" with our kids (and grandkids) are incredibly important and something they will never forget!

Donna remembers,

> *My dad had a great sense of humor and would allow his girls*
> *to "do his hair," when we were little, sitting on the floor, and*
> *getting right down there with us to play or wrestle with us. His*
> *laugh was infectious, and if he told us a joke, he could hardly*
> *get it out as he would roar with laughter!*

It has often been said of me that I truly celebrate life in all circumstances, and my son, Micah, is like me in this. My daughter-in-law, Brooke, has sometimes said she has four kids (imagine a smiling emoji) because Micah is such a "kid at heart" alongside their other three. He is so like his granddaddy and me, determined to focus on the good in others and celebrate life with those he loves. Celebrating life means truly celebrating people—celebrating who God created them to be and finding joy in all of God's good gifts. Through the years with his three children, I have seen Micah build tree houses and zip lines, hike for geocache treasures, play video games, read books, build countless Lego sets, ride mountain bikes, go camping, and play cars on the floor for hours. Micah has taught his kids to notice the stars in the sky, survive while camping, and snowboard down a mountain. He has spent countless hours building a teepee out of sticks and a dirt bike course in their backyard which also sports a zipline! Our whole family loves going to the latest movie, and he has made this a priority in his schedule.

Each of Micah's children attest to the special time and attention Micah has spent with them. Micah's youngest son, Ben, loves watching shows like Mandalorian with his dad and going on adventures with him. He has his dad's playful spirit and is so grateful for the time Micah spends coaching his golf club team as well as lead a Bible study for his friends.

Micah's oldest, Jaden, who has enjoyed all those fun experiences with Micah when he was younger and today probably most enjoys skiing together, describes his dad as "a loving man who can find joy in just about every situation. He puts the needs of others before himself. *He's what I hope to be as a dad when I have my own family.*" As a parent reading this, you would probably agree with me those words are the greatest gift a child can give their parent.

Myla, her daddy's "Butterfly," says,

> *My dad is the light that is needed in the world. He is the joy that puts smiles on faces, especially mine and he doesn't hesitate to help. He will be the last person playing ball with us when everyone else is already done! My dad is a good dad, but even more than being a good dad, he is my friend, and he makes me feel safe. He's someone I can say anything to, and he never shares an opinion that prevents me from sharing mine because his mind is open and free, accepting me. Jesus told us to live like him and to live for him and that is exactly what my dad does. He is a walking example of how God shows us to behave. My dad's spirit is kind and gentle. There is no room left for harm because his mind is pure. He has shown me how to make friends because he makes friends everywhere he goes.*

Jaden, as a child, loved building forts and racing bikes alongside his dad, and today is following in his father's footsteps into ministry. And *that* is the greatest gift Micah has given his children: like Myla said, he has modeled how to walk closely with our *heavenly* Father and how to serve God with all our heart. ***He has shown them that celebrating life means celebrating and serving the One who gave you that life.***

It probably goes without saying that my own daddy was the greatest example to me of how to celebrate life. Life with my dad was spent in places like Disneyland and camping in gorgeous settings like Yellowstone Park and the Rocky Mountains. It was playing games and watching fun old television shows like the original "Addams Family." (Another smiling emoji!) He told the corniest jokes and was always making me laugh. But most importantly, as I mentioned before, he taught me how to live by Philippians 4, that no matter what was happening in my life, if I chose to focus on what was still "excellent and praiseworthy," God would give me his peace. When I experienced a difficult time in my life, his example saved me emotionally. My spiritual mentor, Char, once said to me, "I am amazed that even when your heart is broken, you are still able to celebrate life." Thank you, Daddy, for giving me the gift of living by Philippians 4.

If you are a dad reading this, I hope you will take the time to read the chapters written for moms because the same truths apply to you. They go further into depth on some of the life challenges that come up while we parent and give specific examples of how parents just like you have overcome those challenges. The stories highlight real parents with real struggles who, with the help of God, learned not just to survive but thrive, and their children alongside them. You are on the most amazing and challenging journey a man can take, impacting children who will pass on what you have taught and modeled for them for generations to come. As my daddy would often pray for me, I pray for you: **May God "bless you and keep you" as you seek to be the merciful father your children need.** (Numbers 6:24)

Chapter 8: Merciful Mothering Celebrates Life

"Oh, give thanks to the LORD, for He is good!
For His mercy endures forever."

1 Chronicles 16:34 (NKJV)

Although the Scriptures don't speak specifically about Jesus "celebrating life," or his sense of humor, it does tell of the many times he enjoyed food and fellowship with his disciples and friends at wedding banquets or dinner parties. From these, we can assume that Jesus did indeed celebrate life. If he felt all our emotions as the Scriptures imply, then we can hypothesize that he laughed and often enjoyed his time spent with those close to him. This enjoyment is closely related to his mercy, which means enjoying life is for you too.

Let me explain: In God's goodness, Jesus offered mercy to everyone around him. Because we can always count upon the gift of his goodness, expressed through his mercy, it frees us to truly enjoy life with our children. The giving of mercy is motivated out of the freedom from condemnation that we ourselves received. Because God's mercy is forever accessible to us, he expects us to offer mercy consistently. Rather than it being a burden, giving mercy becomes our expression of gratitude for the mercy given to us. Giving mercy is at the core of celebrating life! It is so positively oriented, as it offers grace, forgiveness, and love. It chooses again and again to see the good and believe the best. When Philippians 4 says to "rejoice in the Lord," **mercy gives us reason to.**

To "rejoice in the Lord" also applies to the gifts he has given us—to find joy in the children he has entrusted to us. I tended to be the kind of mom who didn't get ruffled by my kids' behavior. You could have called me a "fun" mom. Always encouraging my children to explore and be creative, I gave them freer rein than some moms did. I have always had an energetic, playful spirit (think Otter, Enneagram 7, Influencer, and/or Extrovert depending upon which personality inventory you take), so I decided early on that life was meant to be fun with and for my kids.

There were times when I'm sure my peers thought I was a little crazy. When Micah was less than two years old, I enrolled him in a toddler's art class at the local YMCA. One day, the project was finger-painting, so all the kids put their papers on the table and began applying the gooey paint. Micah also started out that way, but quickly became fascinated with the paint itself and started to explore. Moving from the paper to his arms, he began painting himself.

Any mom in their right mind would have gently corrected their child and directed them to the paper, but I didn't want to squelch his creative spirit! So, I removed his shirt, and Micah proceeded to paint his entire upper body and face while the other moms just stared at us as if I had lost my mind. This towheaded child of mine was now green with just his white hair sticking up. He looked like the Grinch, and I probably told him so! When class ended, with arms outstretched, I gingerly carried Micah into the public restroom and stood him in the sink where I began washing away the green paint.

Throughout his childhood, we encouraged Micah's creativity by enrolling him in art classes. We framed his and Maren's art and it still hangs on our walls today. He probably has no conscious memory of the finger-paint incident, but Micah spent a significant chunk of his adult life as a graphic designer before going into vocational youth ministry, and his artistic gifts are very much a part of who he is. Mercy in his life meant expecting the best of him and enabling him to develop and celebrate the gifts God had given him.

Celebrating God's forever mercy in my son's and daughter's childhoods also meant laughing when I really wanted to cry. As I mentioned in the first chapter, Maren, three years younger than Micah, treated sleep as if it were a curse; she avoided it like the plague. No matter what I tried, she hated to go to sleep, and once she fell asleep, didn't remain there long! She was almost five years old before she began sleeping well through the night. I remember when Micah was born, feeling as a first-time mom that I would never have the opportunity to sleep again—that I would *always* be tired.

But I didn't really know what "tired" meant until Maren was born. One night, when she was barely three years old, we had friends over to visit. Like her mommy, Maren was a "people person," so this made going to bed, away from our friends, even more of a necessary evil—a thing to be avoided. I tried for a couple hours to help her settle down. Finally, frustrated, and tired, I thought I had accomplished getting her to fall asleep. I walked out of her bedroom and with exasperated arms waving, told our friends I had succeeded. To my dismay and surprise, they burst out laughing, telling me that not only was Maren walking directly behind me, but she was mimicking every movement I was making!

In moments like this, one has the choice to either laugh or cry. I tell friends that the most difficult thing for me about having children was lack of sleep; I was *so* tired! As tired as I felt, it would have been easy to cry. But it really *was* funny, so I chose to laugh and march her gently back to bed. We have the choice, at any given moment in life, to react with anger and bitterness or choose to rejoice in our circumstances and offer mercy. **Although it is not always easy, choosing mercy is the better way, which ultimately leads to peace of mind and heart.**

There is such incredible comfort that comes from knowing we can always depend upon God's mercy, expressed to us through the unending, all-encompassing mercy of Jesus. No matter what we do, we can trust him to be merciful, forgive us, and believe the best about us. **He so desires that we have his same heart of mercy toward our children and find joy in the life he has given us with them.** Jesus had such an amazingly open heart toward children because he understood that, in their innocence, they were able to freely embrace his love. When he commanded the disciples to let the children come to him, he modeled to us the truth that children are meant to be celebrated rather than seen as an inconvenience or lived on the sidelines. Jesus commanded, "'You must let little children come to me—never stop them! For the kingdom of God belongs to such as these. Indeed, I assure you that the man who does not accept the kingdom of God like a little child will never enter it.' Then he took the children in his arms and laid his hands on them and blessed them" (Mark 10:15-16 J.B. PHILLIPS). Jesus so highly revered the trusting heart of a child that he held them up as an example for us to follow!

As Creator, he knew full well that sometimes their example was anything but perfect. At times, being merciful and celebrating life with our kids means having a sense of humor in situations that make us want to cry or get angry. I imagine Jesus shaking his head and chuckling over my stubbornness because he truly knows what is best for me—and I just haven't figured it out yet.

Once, my friend Lisa came to visit me in California, and we took her kids to Legoland. Amusement parks can make for a very long day for kids. Often, the places we think they will enjoy the most become the perfect environment for tantrums because there is simply too much stimulus and not enough rest!

Walking through the park gift shop, I spotted a princess cape I thought Lisa's daughter, Alexis, might like to try on. Without thinking, I placed it on her, forgetting to consider that she might decide she "had to have it." When Lisa tried to put it back on the rack, Lexi began screaming. Calmly reasoning with her went out the window as she proceeded to throw herself to the ground and roll down the sloping sidewalk. Obviously, everyone around us was staring at this comical, outrageous display. Lisa and I weren't quite sure what to do, so we just laughed to each other and at the situation as Lexi rolled away from us.

Lisa could have overreacted in anger and made Alexis even more upset. Instead, putting herself in Lexi's place, trying to understand her frustration and disappointment—no matter how melodramatic it seemed to us—Lisa was able to stay calm and offer Lexi the merciful response she needed to eventually relax. She didn't get the cape, but she also didn't feel condemned for her childish response. We were able to go on and enjoy our day with the kids, and many years later we still laugh about this experience.

Celebrating life with your child also means accepting who God created them to be and understanding their personality. How they receive your love and respond to you will depend greatly upon their personality type. There are so many good resources out there, but my favorites are the older, commonly known ones by Gary Smalley because he makes it so easy to visualize what this all means. If a "lion" father scolds his "golden retriever" little girl, he needs to consider her tender, gentle spirit. A playful "otter" mother needs to respect that her careful "beaver" son functions best with order and a schedule, which might be a challenge for her. In the reverse, a "beaver" dad might need to let go of his schedule to spontaneously go and have fun with his kids! I encourage you to learn more about personality types, who you are and who your children are, so you can honor them as God created them to be. This frees you to "meet your child where they are at."

I began writing this book on parenting many years ago but put it aside to focus on our marriage ministry, creating a curriculum for The Significant Marriage, the non-profit organization my husband Dave and I founded. At the time, our four children were all grown, and I had a lot of freedom to be actively involved in this marriage ministry. I even got to meet friends for coffee and travel the world with Dave for his job.

Though I had put it aside, this book on merciful mothering happened to be the first one in which a publisher expressed interest. As such, I planned to pick it back up. Much to my surprise, though, God had a new plan in store for these days. Instead of *writing* about parenting, I got to experience it all over again as a grandparent. While my daughter, Maren, completed graduate school, I took care of her 10-month-old son, Elliot, four days each week, ALL day! In hindsight, I see that God has a way of perfectly organizing our days for his purposes if we trust him. But talk about "life as I knew it" being turned upside down! One day, my daughter-in-law, Brooke, who was expecting her first son, laughed when she said she would be calling me instead of my daughter for baby advice!

As I share in this book what God has taught me about merciful mothering, I am not just remembering the experiences I had with my own children. I was actually living every day the reality of helping raise a grandchild with all the responsibilities, frustrations, challenges, and joys! I was forced to remember daily that this precious child is a gift from the Lord and God was calling me to be merciful in his life. Every time I wanted to get something done and Elliot was demanding my attention, I was reminded that these days will pass too quickly. I chose to relish in the chance to cuddle with him, so thankful that he was a loving child and wanted to be with me. Now that he is a young adult and still one of my best buddies, I am so grateful that I had those busy, fun-filled, sometimes-tiring extra moments with him. Choosing to put aside my needs for his wasn't really a sacrifice, but rather brought me incredible joy.

Anytime I sat at the table and turned to find that Elliot had, in warp speed, taken all the pictures off the bottom of my refrigerator, I had a choice to make. I could either react in frustration or I could offer him mercy. I could choose to understand that he was simply a very busy, curious child, and see the best in him. When he would stiffen his little body so I couldn't strap him into his car seat, I could either get angry at him or try to see the situation through his eyes, understanding that his car seat frustrated his love of always being on the go. I would tell myself, *this little blond, blue-eyed toddler needs my mercy and it is a privilege from the Lord to practice returning to Elliot what God has so graciously given me.* In return, God gave me constant laughter over Elliot's silly antics. Elliot's laugh-out-loud joy each time he saw me and his unconditional love toward me—still to this day—made every tiring, challenging moment worth it. When he was four years old, his adopted sister, Lola Swapna, joined the family, so my joy was even multiplied!

To rejoice in the messy house covered in toys, appreciate the sound of a child's laughter and see the good in them even when you are exasperated, is choosing to mother your kids in the power of mercy. Since Maren and her husband were living with us while she was in graduate school, we were around Elliot all the time. My husband, Dave, had to let go of his need for an orderly home to make room for all of Elliot's baby gear, and I watched him practice mercy in putting Elliot's needs first. The result for him was as much joy as it was for me. I can still see them "toasting" with Elliot's toddler cup and signing "I love you." God calls us to "rejoice" in our children and to celebrate these moments he has given us with them. I look back on those days with such a grateful heart that we had that time together. My "little ones" are now in their forties, married, and have their own teenagers. It is so true that you eventually will wonder where the time went.

When Micah was born years ago, someone gave me a plaque that became my mantra for parenting. *"Quiet down cobwebs. Dust go to sleep. I'm rocking my baby and babies don't keep."* I chose to live by this while my children grew. There was always something to be done but when the park beckoned, we went, when a book called, we read it. There was so much of life to explore: playgrounds to enjoy, museums to visit, ducks to feed, snow-covered hills to sled down. I didn't want to miss a thing with them!

I tried, for the sake of my husband's peace of mind, to keep the house looking neat and comfortable, but it definitely wasn't as clean as it could have been. Looking back on those years and how I chose to spend my time, I am thankful that I was able to rejoice in that season of life that now seems like it was gone in a heartbeat. There were days when I felt overwhelmed and even more days I was so exhausted I could barely see straight. But this legacy the Lord gave me to grow for him has become two incredible adults who call me *friend* as well as *Mom*. When I look back on those too-short years that felt at the time like they would last forever, I find great joy in the memories and am so thankful we were able to celebrate life together. Furthermore, it gives me such joy to watch them celebrating life with their own children.

As I bring this book to a close, I want to leave you with specific encouragement, a "list" if you will, of ways in which you can show mercy to your child. If you only come back to the last few paragraphs of this book, what can you take with you that will be life-giving?

In closing, how does a mom genuinely "give thanks to the Lord" for the children he has given her? **One way is to focus on the Lord's mercies in your own life.** How has the Lord shown his gentleness, forgiveness, and patience to *you*?

Another way is to **live by Philippians 4:4-9, remembering and recording, in a tangible place that you and your children can see, what is good about each of your kids.** As you study this short, but powerful passage of Scripture, you will learn how to **focus on what is praiseworthy about your children** and about this time in their lives. What parts are you thankful for? It may take practice, but it is worth every effort!

Check to **be sure their "emotional love tank" is full.** What have you done this day to ensure they are feeling loved by you in the way they need? Take time to cuddle with your child and **give them your focused attention.** Look them in the eyes when you talk to them. Begin to **experience your children as little persons to be embraced and respected,** just as Jesus embraced the children the disciples wanted to send away.

Laugh when you would rather cry. When your children misbehave or disappoint you, **call down the powers of heaven** when you struggle to offer grace and mercy to them.

Encourage their gifts in every way possible. Help them explore and develop skills using those gifts.

Make the most of these too-fleeting moments that have been given to you, remembering that "babies don't keep."

Jesus knew how to celebrate children, and his mercies extended especially to them. I believe with all my heart that if we practice mercy as he has offered it to us, he will honor our efforts to live as he is calling us to live. If Jesus were a mom, he would have been slow to anger and quick to cuddle. He would have laughed often, forgiven easily, and focused on the good in these little people. Daily, he would have shown humble compassion, placing himself in the heart of a child so that he could embrace their feelings and offer understanding. *As mothers and—for some of us—grandmothers, we can look to Jesus as an example of who we can be if we are faithful to follow his example. With every decision, every action, I want to be a mother like him.*

Making It Personal

Chapter 1 Questions

Merciful Parenting Seeks to be Consistently Compassionate

"The Lord's acts of mercy indeed do not end, for his compassions never fail.

They are new every morning..." Lam. 3:22-23 (NASB) to introduce the questions related to merciful parenting.

What are three ways that I could "see the world" through my child's eyes?

_____

_____

_____

_____

_____

_____

_____

_____

When do I struggle to show compassion?

_____

_____

_____

_____

_____

_____

_____

_____

_____

_____

Do I believe that God is able to help me because He understands my struggles?

_____

_____

_____

_____

_____

_____

_____

I choose to claim that He is able to do through me everything He asks of me!

Chapter 2 Questions

Merciful parenting is humble and kind

"Therefore…clothe yourselves with compassion, kindness, humility, gentleness and patience."

Colossians 3:12 (NIV)

Eye contact, physical affection, focused attention and discipline…

Which of these come easily for me?

_____

_____

_____

_____

_____

_____

_____

Which is more of a challenge?

_____

_____

_____

_____

_____

_____

_____

Which of these means love to my child?

_____

_____

_____

_____

_____

_____

_____

_____

How can I specifically show love to my child?

_____

_____

_____

_____

_____

_____

How can I balance discipline with kind mercy which says, "go and sin no more?"

_____

_____

_____

_____

_____

_____

Chapter 3 Questions

Merciful Parenting Blossoms Out of a Healed Heart

"So let's walk right up to him and get what he is so ready to give.

Take the mercy, accept the help." Hebrews 4:16 (MSG)

When I think of my upbringing, what possibly prevents me from offering mercy at times?

_____

_____

_____

_____

_____

_____

What can I be grateful for in the way I was parented? What do I want to repeat with my own child?

_____

_____

_____

_____

_____

_____

_____

Do I need to find a therapist, a mentor, allowing God to heal my own wounded heart?

_____

_____

_____

_____

_____

_____

_____

_____

What steps can I take toward healing?

_____

_____

_____

_____

_____

_____

_____

_____

_____

Chapter 4 Questions

Merciful Parenting Focuses on the Good

*"Finally, brothers and sisters, whatever is true, whatever
is noble, whatever is right, whatever is pure, whatever is
lovely, whatever is admirable—**if anything** --is excellent or
praiseworthy—think about such things." Philippians 4:8 (NIV)*

What are 3 "excellent and praiseworthy" characteristics of my
child that I can focus on and be grateful for?

_____

_____

_____

_____

_____

_____

_____

_____

_____

_____

_____

_____

_____

_____

Have I ever felt like a fool in front of others with my child? If it happens again, how can I change my focus to the truth of what is STILL good about my child? What can I let go of to allow God to change my heart and see my child thru His eyes?

_____

_____

_____

_____

_____

_____

_____

_____

_____

_____

_____

_____

_____

_____

_____

_____

_____

_____

_____

_____

Chapter 5 Questions

Merciful Parenting Offers Unconditional Love

If you love someone, you will be loyal to him no matter what the cost.

You will always believe in him, always expect the best of him, and always stand your ground in defending him.

1 Corinthians 13:7 (TLB)

Do I have any possibly unrealistic expectations for my child?

_____

_____

_____

_____

_____

_____

_____

_____

How can I love "in spite of" instead of "if" or "because?"

_____

_____

_____

_____

_____

_____

_____

_____

_____

Is there anything I need to let go of with my child and give completely to God?

_____

_____

_____

_____

_____

_____

_____

How can I best balance consequences with merciful forgiveness?

_____

_____

_____

_____

_____

_____

_____

Chapter 6 Questions

Merciful Parenting Forgives What Is Undeserved

"Don't worry over anything whatever; whenever you pray tell God every detail of your needs in earnest and thankful prayer, and the peace of God, which transcends human understanding, will keep constant guard over your hearts and mind as they rest in Christ Jesus." Philippians 4:6-7 (J.B. Phillips New Testament, PHILLIPS)

How can I better "choose my battles" so my child will respond to the most important things?

_____

_____

_____

_____

_____

_____

_____

_____

I believe I could grow in this area (praying for my child, seeking a mentor, be slow to anger, choose kindness, live a life of integrity)

_____

_____

_____

_____

_____

_____

_____

_____

_____

How can I specifically choose to be more merciful, as Jesus is merciful toward me?

_____

_____

_____

_____

_____

_____

_____

Do I need to lay my child at the feet of Jesus?

_____

_____

_____

_____

_____

_____

_____

Chapter 7 Questions

Merciful Fathering

"Be completely humble and gentle; be patient, bearing with one another in love."

Ephesians 4:2 (NIV)

As a dad, what are three ways I could focus on the good in my child?

_____

_____

_____

_____

_____

_____

_____

_____

_____

How could I celebrate life more with my child and see the world through their eyes?

_____

_____

_____

_____

_____

_____

_____

_____

_____

_____

_____

_____

Does my heart need to be healed so that I can love my children with merciful love? What steps will I take to make this happen?

_____

_____

_____

_____

_____

_____

_____

_____

_____

_____

_____

Chapter 8 Questions

Merciful Mothering Celebrates Life

"Give thanks to the Lord for He is good, for his mercy endures forever!"

1 Chronicles 16:34 (NIV)

To think about....

Do I find joy in my child?

_____

_____

_____

Am I able to laugh when I'd rather cry?

_____

_____

_____

Could offering mercy give me more peace of mind?

_____

_____

_____

What would it take for me to be able to truly rejoice in my child?

_____

_____

_____

In looking at "Parenting Choices to Live By" (see the following page) *what are four I could focus on,* allowing God to change my heart and help me celebrate my child? (These might be different for each child if you have more than one)

Parenting Choices to Live By

Focus on the Lord's mercies in your own life

Live by Philippians 4:4-9 focusing on what is praiseworthy

Look your child in the eyes

Experience them as little persons to be embraced and respected

Laugh when you could cry

Call down the powers of heaven

Be sure your child's "emotional love tank" is full

Encourage their gifts

Make the most of these moments that are fleeting

Be slow to anger and quick to cuddle